PASTOR

THOUGHT you would ENJOY
THIS BOOK. I APPRECIATE
You so MUCH GLAD
YOUR MY PASTOR
GOD BLESS you ALWAYS

YOUR SECRET PAL

July 1988

REDISCOVERING THE CHARISMATA

Building Up the
Body of Christ
through Spiritual Gifts

REDISCOVERING THE CHARISMATA

Charles V. Bryant

WORD BOOKS
PUBLISHER
WACO, TEXAS

A DIVISION OF
WORD, INCORPORATED

Library of Congress Cataloging in Publication Data

Bryant, Charles V., 1930–
  Rediscovering the charismata.

  Bibliography: p.
  1. Gifts, Spiritual.   I. Title.
BT767.3.B77   1986   234'.13   85–30414
ISBN 0–8499–0539–7

Printed in the United States of America
6 7 8 9 8 BKC 9 8 7 6 5 4 3 2 1

To
Wanda, my wife
Jayne, Donna, Charma, and Juanita, my daughters
B.J. Lewis, my secretary
and
Carey Moore, my editor

Contents

CONTENTS

Foreword

WE ARE EXPERIENCING a plethora of books in the so-called charismatic movement; a few are critical, most are appreciative and commendatory, but not many are objective and analytical. Most of the books have come out of the movement itself and therefore display the thought of its protagonists and devotees.

This book is written from a wider perspective. The author is not a critic of the charismatic movement. Neither is he a charismatic in the sense that he is a member either of a Pentecostal church or of some defined fellowship of charismatics within a given denomination. He plays the part of a philosophic onlooker, observing what he takes to be a formidable movement within Christendom and seeking to understand and elucidate its principles by explicating their sources in the New Testament, defining their meaning in terms of contemporary thought, and—especially—showing their value and applicability. Today, indeed, this is by all odds the best book on the gifts of the Spirit that I have had the privilege of reading. The research underlying it is solid and dependable. The power of analysis is keen and discerning. And the suggestions for adoption and general use by the membership of the church are wise, practical, and spiritually edifying.

The book enumerates twenty-seven gifts of the Spirit, insisting that all of the gifts are proffers of divine grace. One can't choose for himself or herself just any gift and cultivate it. A gift comes to the person from the hands of God, who takes the initiative in the transaction. But, once given by God, it is up to the individual as to how that gift will be used and what effect it will have in his or her life and in the lives of others.

In this book, Charles Bryant distinguishes between talents, that is, attributes of nature such as intelligence, physical stamina, health, and the like, and the superior personal spiritual gifts, which though they correspond in many instances to their natural counterparts, are nevertheless distinct and different and reach us from an outside source. They are not indigenous to our being.

He likewise shows the difference between fruits of the Spirit and gifts of the Spirit, a most important distinction in the development of the Christian life.

This inspiring book should be read, not by a single group within the church, but by all Christians. It can be instructive and edifying to all seekers of the truth in Christ Jesus and sincere servants of the living Lord.

Bishop William R. Cannon
The United Methodist Church
Atlanta, Georgia

Introduction

JOHN NAISBITT OPENS *Megatrends* with the statement, "As a society, we have been moving from the old to the new. And we are still in motion. Caught between eras, we experience turbulence. Yet, amid the sometimes painful and uncertain present, the restructuring of America proceeds unrelentingly."

Naisbitt was not only describing our country, but also the institutions that make up the country. The church is one of them. It, too, is "moving from the old to the new." To be sure, there is "turbulence" whenever anything begins moving, but the turbulence we are experiencing in the church is healthy and growth-producing. That health and growth is what this book will consider.

One source of turbulence in the church is the rediscovery of the large number of people whose lives we are not touching, both outside and inside the church. Even with all the television programs and networks that are declared to be Christian, some 2.5 billion people in the world have no way of being introduced to the message and ministry of

Christ through current ways or means. And this group is growing daily.

These are not the only persons in need of the message of salvation entrusted to us. A vast and growing number of people within our own memberships and constituencies are not being touched. One report by the Princeton Religion Research Center and the Gallup Organization, Inc., indicates that this bloc of people claim to believe in God, the Bible, and in Jesus Christ. But what is missing for them is that "most churches are not effective in helping people to find meaning in life . . . most churches have lost the real spiritual part of religion."

That looks fairly negative; but in reality, this spiritual need poses as a challenge that thrusts us into the struggle and requires that we be more than what we are, and do more than what we think we can. In light of the condition of the churches, I am proposing a serious study of the extraordinary powers God gives to people who receive the Holy Spirit. These powers are manifestly present in the discovery, development, and deployment of spiritual gifts by which we are able to be more (in the Spirit) than what we are (in the flesh) and to do more (in the Spirit) than what we can (in the flesh).

The past two years have been the most exciting ones of my thirty-year ministry as I have been privileged to conduct some one hundred workshops and seminars on spiritual gifts (charismata). I am realizing how open and eager Christians are to discover and claim ministries that are designed by God for them.

Unfortunately, in the mainline churches this study of specific gifts for ministry has not had the attention that could have made our history different. But that is changing in this "moving from the new to the old." I see a new "early church" awakening, not as we thought it would happen some three or four decades ago through revivals and decisions for Christ, but in a deeper exposure to and study of the manifestations of the Holy Spirit and the charismatic structuring of church ministries.

Let me illustrate this. I have been able to find only one book on the subject of spiritual gifts published before 1972. That book, *Concerning Spiritual Gifts*, was written by a British Pentecostal in 1928 and has since been reprinted by the Gospel Publishing House in the United States. Since 1972, scores of books have been published on the subject, mainly by non-Pentecostal authors and publishing houses.

During the 1950s something happened. But before we attempt to describe it, perhaps we need a brief background. The early period of the New Testament church was one with vital expressions of effective ministry, structured by the free and directive power of the Holy Spirit. Under the Holy Spirit's direction and gifting, the church was a highly visible community-type organism, one made up of complementary and harmonizing parts; but parts which were distinctively and functionally different. Paul directed his attention to these different parts or gifts in Romans 12, 1 Corinthians 12, and Ephesians 4, and he did so mainly because of prevailing ignorance and abuse of the gifts. He never made any effort to justify or defend the charismata.

Subsequent history shows us how far Christians drifted from the direct endowment of the Holy Spirit. While the early church was made up of Spirit-filled or endowed persons, by the end of the first century a division began to be apparent. A priesthood of special persons dominated an unpriestly laity, the former having special qualities and privileges granted under the authority of institutional leaders. This, despite the New Testament teaching that the whole new people of God is a priesthood ministering to one another for edification and the whole body ministering to the whole world.

The charismatic structuring for edification (building up)

and mission (outreach) began to erode severely when a clear-cut division between clergy and laity became official toward the end of the second century. Intrigue toward the Holy Spirit and the "experience" of his empowering gave way to doctrines, creeds, and theologies about the Holy Spirit. This prevailed until the sixteenth century when a new breakthrough came as the result of personal conversion and the enlightenment of the Holy Spirit. Assailed by the explosive force of this "new wine," church organizational structures swayed and tottered and gave way to new churches coming to birth, the Bible replaced dusty creeds, and men wrote new theologies. It was nothing less than a Reformation. Its authentic spiritual power spread throughout the whole church, as the church, in the following centuries, spread out to the whole world with the good news.

A more recent and significant result was that sometime in the 1950s this all came to an apex when laypeople of all cultures, races, and denominations suddenly became aware that they were not second-class citizens in God's kingdom. Something happened to them that could only be explained as an outpouring of God's Spirit. And with that Spirit, certain extraordinary spiritual powers became manifest. To be sure, this was not confined to laypersons. Pastor and priest also realized new power. It came to the attention of all that the special graces did not belong only to an ordained clergy.

By the 1970s, such a wind was blowing—at first called Neo-Pentecostalism and then the "charismatic movement"—that many church leaders and pastors began to open themselves to the possibility of something far beyond just another religious fad. A new hope for "meaning in life" and the "real spiritual part of religion" was born.

This new hope lay in the rediscovery that God's people are one. All members of the body of Christ are to be treated and respected with equal charismatic ranking, never as one over another but all as servants in ministry to and with everyone else (Rom. 12:3–5).

When people open themselves to God, they find that an experience of the Spirit of God is inseparable from the discovery and exercise of the charismata, the gifts. Such should never be a threat to any church body that seeks to lift up the church as the body of Christ in and for the world. Nor should the exercise of the gifts threaten any church official.

We are increasingly aware of a charismatic renewal growing within the mainline churches. And where this is happening, new vigor and growth are taking place. The charismatic movement of the 1950s is not going away. We must not want it to leave because of what is happening as a result. Laypersons are experiencing the reality of the Spirit in their lives in such a way that peculiar abilities and power for Christian services are surfacing. They are viewing this new experience as gifts for ministry, not as an opportunity to display and engage in emotional "orgies" as was reported in some quarters during the initial phase of the movement.

It has been my observation while conducting workshops on spiritual gifts that most Christians are, indeed, looking for more than a deliverance from sin and guilt. They want to know how they can best serve the church, the body of Christ. They want to be a source of new life and effectiveness for the church. As they have become exposed to Paul's teachings on "spiritual things" (1 Cor. 12:1) or "gifts" (Rom. 12:6 and Eph. 4:8–11), they have discovered with great excitement that there was available to them a definitive gift or gifts (charismata). These gifts, they realized, are not reserved for a special class of ordained and institutionally appointed ministers, but for everyone. They discovered that all Christians share in "spiritual things" (*pneumatikos*); that there is legitimacy in desiring spiritual gifts (1 Cor. 12:31), not for self-glory or aggrandizement, but for the "common good" and "upbuilding of the body of Christ" (Eph. 4:12).

This discovery of an ability given by God has elevated them. They are now aware that they share a significant partnership with others in ministry (*diakonia*). They have learned what joyful experiences awaited their acts of obedience in employing their spiritual gifts for others (1 Pet. 4:10), and have discovered that within the body of Christ the gifts for ministry are different but equally ranked in importance (Eph. 4:11–16) and function; that the source of all gifts for ministry is God's grace-filled act of assigning and distributing the gifts according to his will and their receptivity; and that all this was not based on natural qualities, training, talents, circumstances, or institutional ordinations, but rather on God's choosing and gifting (1 Cor. 12:11).

In these many workshops and seminars on spiritual gifts I have witnessed the joy of these discoveries and the effectiveness for service that followed. Some who were "burned out" became spiritually alive. Churches have become influential as the members find their places for ministry designed and given by God. New hope and vision are taking over the lives of pastors who are discovering their spiritual gifts.

It is my earnest hope as you read the following pages that you will fully open yourself to the possibilities of a new ordering of ministry and direction for life under the power and guidance of the Holy Spirit. May we all become willing to learn what the Spirit has to say, to receive what the Spirit has to offer, and to do what the Spirit has equipped us to do. The present may appear to be painful and uncertain, but the restructuring of the church is proceeding "unrelentingly."

REDISCOVERING THE CHARISMATA

1

The Meaning of Spiritual Gifts

FOUR BIBLICAL PASSAGES definitely deal with spiritual gifts or charismata. They are found in Romans 12:1–8, 1 Corinthians 12:1–31, Ephesians 4:1–16, and 1 Peter 4:10, 11. These are radically different textually and contextually, yet all form a unity of meaning and objectivity which cement together authenticity and effectiveness in the church's ministry to itself—edification—and, through itself, to all people. In these passages, which list some twenty spiritual gifts, certain principles become vividly noticeable:

1. *The gifts are given for the purpose of use.* The gifts are not for adornment or status, not for power or popularity, but are to be used in service to the body of Christ, the church, and through the church to the world.

The biblical word is *diakonia,* meaning service. And not service in just any sense, but service that is given in agape love. First Peter 4:10 says, "As each has received a gift, employ it for one another . . . in order that in everything God may be glorified through Jesus Christ." First Corinthians 12:7 says, "To each is given the manifestation of the Spirit for the common good (*sympheron*)." Ephesians 4:11, 12 says, "And his gifts were . . . for building up the body of Christ. . . ."

The principle here is that the gifts are given, and given for a purpose beyond our own choosing. They are not to be considered personal property or natural qualities, but as energies provided by the Holy Spirit, energies that form boundaried functions or ministries for and through the body. This is where authenticity and effectiveness are provided for in the fellowship or *koinonia* of Christians, the body of Christ.

2. *The gifts are assigned, appointed, given, and energized by God.* While we may desire certain gifts, as a person may desire to be taller or have more hair but cannot do anything about it, there is no guaranteed acquisition. A misunderstanding has occurred at this point because of an unfortunate translation of 1 Corinthians 12:31. It appears that Paul is setting the reader up for the possibility and legitimacy of desiring or aiming for certain "higher gifts." In the Greek language, however, the verb that is translated "desire" or "aim at" can be translated as either in the indicative or imperative mood. No rule except the context governs the translation. Unfortunately, an early translator chose the imperative form and others apparently followed suit. However, in view of the real problem Paul was addressing among the Corinthian Christians, their invidious and self-seeking exercise of the gifts, it would be more consistent with the contextual problems to translate "desire" or "aim at" in the indicative. This would change the whole mood of the sentence and would come out like this: "So you desire the higher gifts! Well, I'll show you the highest of them all." Then Paul launches into his inimitable examination of agape love.

This explanation is in concert with the other related passages: "Having gifts that differ according to the grace *given* to us . . ." (Rom. 12:6, italics added); ". . . but it is the same God who *inspires* them all in every one" (1 Cor. 12:6, italics added); "All these are inspired by one and the same Spirit, who *apportions* to each one individually as he wills" and "God has *appointed* in the church . . ." (1 Cor. 12:11, 28, italics added).

The point here is that God makes the choice, not the individual or the community of Christians. God is the creator of the fellowship (2 Corinthians 13:14) within which the various gifts for service are assigned. God alone knows what is needed for the "upbuilding of the body of Christ" and the "common good" of the church.

We all sense the importance of the above fact. But how do we or can we give over our big, impersonal institution— the denomination—to such a dynamic and unpredictable force as the Holy Spirit? This is the question that haunts us. And we have not always been able to cope with our own attempts to resist or sidestep the power and guidance of the Holy Spirit. Out of confusion, perhaps even distrust, about the dynamics of the Spirit's presence, it may be that we often find it easier to continue doing what we've always done than to open ourselves for a fresh outpouring of God's Spirit.

Current needs, however, and spiritual powers have always been the active agenda of the Holy Spirit. This is why it is so important for the church to be open to assignments, appointments, and charges from God. There is no other way for us to get back to, or move forward to, the unity and bond of fellowship that is unique to the intimate reality of the body of Christ. Paul said it in 1 Corinthians 1:7–9: "There is indeed no single gift you lack, while you wait expectantly for our Lord Jesus Christ to reveal himself. He will keep you firm to the end, without reproach on the

Day of our Lord Jesus. It is God himself who called you to share in the life of his Son Jesus Christ our Lord; and God keeps faith" (NEB).

3. *The spiritual gifts are for everyone.* No one is excluded from receiving a gift/s. The gifts are given to everyone individually and to the church as a community. Paul makes much of this connectedness and corporateness in fellowship with the Spirit. The principle is: to each, with and for all; everything and all for the glory of God.

Paul found the Corinthians moving from disunity to anarchy in the uses and abuses of the various gifts. He immediately addressed this condition by explaining the unity of the gifts *in* Christ and the use of them *under* Christ's lordship. All gifts are to be regarded as essential to the body of Christ and all are made active through individuals, but only through the persons who practice their gifts unselfishly for the benefit of the church worldwide (1 Cor. 12:12, 27).

4. *There is an unlimited variety of gifts.* This is not to suggest the scene of persons standing in a line at a cafeteria of charismata and that we may choose according to our delights. Paul makes it clear that the gifts are grace-given, issuing out of God's choices and designs. It is obvious, furthermore, in the four biblical passages mentioned that there is no limit to the number of gifts. The only limitation comes from our resistance to and rejection of the Holy Spirit (1 Thess. 5:19; Eph. 4:30).

The different listings of the gifts in the four passages suggest strongly that in Paul's mind, at least, and perhaps in the minds of those to whom he was writing, it wasn't necessary to mention every conceivable gift. It is apparent to me that Paul mainly mentioned two categories of gifts: the gifts the Corinthians were abusing, and those being overlooked, if not altogether ignored. The Corinthians were limiting themselves to the so-called spectacular or sensational gifts, that is, tongues, miracles, healings, and prophecy.

We can imagine what a shock it was when Paul began to mention other gifts such as interpretation of tongues, discerning of spirits, wisdom, knowledge, helps, and administration. These, you see, had lost status and intrigue in the midst of emotional ecstasies and dramatic miracles.

To be sure, there was no lack of enthusiasm over the use of some gifts among the Corinthians. And it is interesting to note that it obviously did not occur to Paul to tell them that the gifts they were using were wrong. But he did score them heavily and sarcastically over their ignorance and negligence of the quieter and often more obscure gifts which were just as essential, if not more so, to the fullness of Christian fellowship and ministry (1 Cor. 12:22–25).

This point becomes even more striking and impressive when we switch from the setting in Corinth of Christians in a local assembly to a broader spectrum such as found in Romans 12. Here we find it very difficult to determine the end of Paul's list of gifts. And it is even more impressive to see how Paul drives on to mention qualities of Christian living that cannot be limited to pulpit "performances" and power positions in the local church. He is speaking to all members of the church.

In Ephesians Paul takes the teaching about gifts beyond Romans and Corinthians to the ultimate. He declares that the purpose of gifts is to bring the church into full maturity in Christ. There is no way for this to be accomplished among disconnected individuals or within a corporate body that overlooks the necessary health and quality of the individuals who make up the body.

5. *The gifts are given for growth and maturity.* The church is a single organism made up of many organs. Each organ has its unique size, shape, position, and function. The health of the whole body is dependent upon the health and proper functioning of the individual parts. The whole

body can never afford to neglect or discount the position and function of any organ—large or small, in close proximity or far from the head. And no individual part, in order to maintain equilibrium and purpose, function and productivity, can overlook the value of the whole body.

Christ is the head of the body, Paul emphasizes, fitting and connecting the individual parts, making them coequal in value but different in function, and thus enabling the body to sustain growth as it builds itself up in love (Eph. 4:11–16).

To summarize all of the principles is to say that Paul's metaphorical use and vision of the church as the body of Christ includes a commission by God, a purpose for service, a balance of interdependent members, and the enabling power of the Spirit's manifestation, all aiming at maturity and wholeness in Christ. He sets before us the challenge of a deepened fellowship, an active and effective every-member ministry, and a maturation process through living faithfully by the standard of love (1 Cor. 13).

Spiritual, Physical, Psychological, and Social Meanings

A holistic understanding of man teaches us that he is not divided into parts, such as mentioned above. These are merely broad categories of meanings that can help us relate man to himself, to God, and to his environment. It would be unfair to rank these in importance unless we are considering one facet for a study. We all know how extremely important each is and how the quality of life is determined by a proper balance of attention given to all four.

Without question, however, many view with high suspicion any study of most anything pertaining to the spiritual aspect of religion and the psychology of human personality.

This is so mainly because of the rapid achievements in the physical sciences. Although the physical sciences are still in their infancy, we in the Western world tend to subordinate nearly everything to them, even psychology and religion.

The church in Western society sold out to this world view that came from Aristotle and was firmed up as a church view by Thomas Aquinas. Simply put, in its practical application, this world view hardly accepts anything that purports to come from or be influenced by a nonphysical realm of existence. This is one reason the church has had a rough time dealing with and sorting out what it believes about the Holy Spirit, a purely spiritual power or influence that manifests itself in the physical.

The physicalistic world view attempts to reduce all events to lawful interactions of matter and energy within a spatio-temporal context. Outside of this, nothing else deserves attention. Furthermore, this approach says that ultimately and inevitably all so-called religious "experiences" can and probably will be measured as mere physical forces within a person's nervous system. In some quarters this is carried further with the suggestion that when a person has a profound, life-changing experience with God (conversion), it is conceivable that an electrode applied to a certain spot on the brain could just as easily have produced the same results. For a long time now, some psychologists have claimed that certain psychochemical drugs could produce and sustain any and all such "spiritual" states normally and historically associated with a nonphysical force source—the grace of God.

The argument in favor of this view depends upon what modern science—physical sciences still in their infancy—has discovered and has been able to achieve. This is not so convincing when we consider the real and potential dangers and devastations science and technology have already imposed on the human race. This, however, is not the place to enter into that debate. Some day, under the grace of God, I expect we will come to understand that it is out of ignorance that we divide man with these artificial categories, and that because of such compartmentalization, ill health—physical, mental, and social—is inevitable. Furthermore, I believe wisdom—*sophia,* one of the spiritual gifts—when discovered and developed, will reveal to us just how unitary we are, although carrying features which may differ qualitatively and quantitatively. Until that day, it is important for us to use what understanding we have with a prayer and a hope that God will indeed become an intimate reality to each of us—" 'in whom we live, move and have our being' " (Acts 17:28).

What we are studying as gifts of the Spirit is what thousands of years of history have been unable to eradicate, although some of man's strongest and most energetic efforts have been put forth in the attempt. The remaining facts are:

- basically and fundamentally man is responding to God who created him and who wishes to have fellowship with him.
- man's chief aim in life is to worship and to glorify God.
- man is not fully man without a conscious awareness of God and a related response of obedience.
- the *pneumatikon* (spiritual things), of which Paul writes in 1 Corinthians 12:1, are those acts of obedience whereby the Christian willingly subsumes his or her physical, psychological, and social aspects of human life under his or her highest nature, the "spiritual" (John 4:24).

By "spiritual" I mean that man's real source of existence is of a realm that cannot be measured by or described with physical means. In the prologue to his Gospel, John attempts to explain where the spiritual life originates. But basically and ultimately about all we can do is to describe the behavioral *responses* to an encounter with God who is spirit.

So Christian man is a spiritual being—in touch with an unseen reality that offers an experience that brings new life, new meanings, and fulfillment. The "spirituals" Paul speaks of in 1 Corinthians 12 are these new meanings and fulfillment. The word he uses here is *pneumatikon,* derived from the root word *pneuma,* the word for spirit. The suffix indicates a plurality or variety of experiences with the Spirit. (I will use the capital form, Spirit, when referring to God.) And these experiences or manifestations are only possible for those who are in touch with the nonphysical realm. He is immanent and transcendent.

Paul goes on to say that the unspiritual person, that is, one who denies or rejects God who is revealed in Jesus Christ, cannot comprehend the spiritual things or gifts of the Spirit (1 Cor. 2:14). The gifts are only for persons who have accepted Jesus Christ as the true source of life: ". . . whom God made our wisdom, our righteousness and sanctification and redemption . . ." (1 Cor. 1:30). Taking this further, there is a special wisdom and understanding the spiritual man has about himself and his life that no amount of this world's wisdom can offer or alter. Even our speaking and explaining of such cannot be comprehended by those whose source of real living is not Jesus Christ. This is one reason for the great gap between the purists in the physicalistic world view and those (some of whom are scientists) who view reality in terms of being "in Christ."

Yet, even the spiritual man cannot divorce himself from the boundaries and limitations of his physical makeup— his psychologial and social characteristics and connections. He doesn't try if he is truly the spiritual man about whom Paul speaks. What he experiences as the "spiritual" transcends a line drawn between spirit and matter. The spiritual gifts themselves demonstrate the intimate relationship between the physical aspects of the human body and mind, spirit, and soul.

Furthermore, it is important to realize that a person's behavior, attitude, outlook, and basic motivations are unavoidably affected by the acknowledged presence of a spiritual gift or gifts. Many members of the body of Christ practice and demonstrate their gifts without being consciously aware of even possessing them. Yet, when the same persons discover that what they have possessed and have been practicing in service to God are, indeed, especially assigned or given gifts for ministry, they become even more energized, intentional, and effective in their services.

I saw this happen at the close of one of my workshops on spiritual gifts. A man of some seventy or more years of age gave a very emotional testimony of what happened to him while shaving that morning. He said, "All my life I knew there was something that I really enjoyed doing for Christ and the church. But I've always had a tinge of guilt, thinking that I was doing my thing for self-satisfaction. This morning, while I was shaving and praying about it all, God revealed to me that what I had been doing and enjoying all along was my gift being expressed. I got so excited about it that I could hardly finish shaving without cutting myself. I've been singing all day long. And to think that I have felt guilty over doing what God wanted me to do!"

The Solution to "Burnout"

Not far from this is the experience many people have had called "burnout," the plague of professions and volunteer organizations. The main cause of burnout in both groups is loss of motivation. When that which motivates a person no longer exists or is too painful to continue to be acknowledged, more energy is required to maintain a

productive level of performance than can be found. Ineffec-
tiveness and escape become paramount problems.

The solution to burnout in the church, for laity and
clergy, is to discover the gift(s) the person has and give
him a place where his gift can be practiced. The gift, you
see, is an endowment of specialized energy from the Holy
Spirit. When this is realized, not only is motivation restored,
but the person also acquires a new self-esteem that is related
to a truly spiritual and biblical basis for his work. A new
confidence about his placeness and function in the body
of Christ motivates him to accept responsibilities without
a sensitivity toward being "used" or "manipulated." His
level of enthusiasm is raised to embrace a positive attitude
toward seemingly impossible odds.

He becomes more than what he is—in the flesh—and
is now able to do more—in the spirit—than what he can.

2

The Source of Spiritual Gifts

ST. PAUL WAS ESPECIALLY GIFTED with the grace of knowledge (*gnōsis*) by which mysteries hidden for ages were revealed (Col. 1:24–29), mysteries concerning Christ's position and operation in God's scheme of salvation offered to the world. In Paul's articulation of some of those mysteries he shares the fact that Christ is to the church as the head is to the human body. In Ephesians Paul indicates that Christ is the giver of the gifts (Eph. 4:7,11); in 1 Corinthians 12 he says that God inspires the gifts and that the manifestations of them are of the Spirit; and in Romans 12 Paul shares with us his understanding of the work of grace as the means by which God gives us the spiritual gifts.

I do not want to dabble here with the trinitarian formula and get caught up in the seemingly interminable profusion of theories and theologies about a triune God. I am not a theologian by training, although I try to think logically about God-man relations. I do find myself in good company when I express an inability to decipher the true relationship between God, Christ, and Holy Spirit.

I have revisited the writings of the Apostolic Fathers, a varied group of writers during the first and second centuries; the Apologists, of the deep second century who vindicated Christianity against the threats and claims of pagans and Jews: the Medieval Theologians, who almost lost the sense of a reasonable experience of anything pertaining to God except that which was institutionalized and approved, if not altogether controlled, by the authority of the church; and the Reformers down to modern theologians, and I found as much of a variety of ideas and confusion among them as I have had in my own understanding or lack of same about the Trinity.

However, the trinitarian aspects of God will not go away. People continue to ask about the origin and distribution of the spiritual gifts we are studying. I simply answer by saying, "According to Scripture, God is the Giver; according to Scripture, Christ is the Giver; and according to Scripture, the Holy Spirit is the Giver." This way, I don't get into too much trouble. And when I am pushed further to explain such a tripartite mystery, my simple and pet way of getting into and out of the difficulty is as follows:

"I am a unitary human being, unable to be divided into parts. Yet, I am a son of my mother and cannot relate to her in any other way than by mother-son relations. I am a husband, and cannot relate to my wife by any other relationship than one as a husband. I am a father of four daughters, and it is impossible for me to relate to them in any other way than in the father-daughter combination. Although I am the same human being through and through, they do not see me as the same. Too, I see myself in three distinctive ways, all three totally different from each other. But I am I and no other—undivided, with the same physical, mental, and emotional equipment in all three roles." Somehow, this helps me to understand God's three basic expressions of himself in what we describe as the Trinity.

What we are studying as spiritual gifts are *new* traits of human behavior that did not exist prior to the "new humanity in Christ" Paul describes in 2 Corinthians 5:17. These gifts do not come through physical birth, genetic transmission, or by education. We are dealing with abilities whose source is spiritual, that is, nonphysical. Our parents did not pass them on to us. Our teachers and coaches did not drill them into our thinking and habits. They are, in Paul's words, *pneumatikon*, things of the Spirit (1 Cor. 12:1, 7).

This does not mean that since the gifts are spiritual things they are strictly from the Third Person of the Trinity. To the contrary, Paul, in many different passages, interchanges the words *God, Christ,* and *Holy Spirit* in reference to the same supernatural or nonphysical power and activity. We do ourselves a confusing disservice to refer to the gifts as esoteric manifestations only of the Spirit (a third person of the Trinity), implying that the Spirit is a force that is subordinate to Christ, while Christ, in second place, is subordinate to and a representative of God. Paul cleared the relationship up by binding all three expressions of God into a whole in 1 Corinthians 12:4–6, thus: "Now there are varieties of gifts (charismata), but the same Spirit (*pneuma*); and there are varieties of service (*diakonia*), but the same Lord; and there are varieties of working (*energemata*), but it is the same God who inspires them all in every one."

Whether we speak of God, Christ, or Holy Spirit, what we are really giving witness to is the transformation of a spiritual nature into a physical presence. We are speaking of an intimacy with God that sheds light on the active presence of a resurrected Christ. We are speaking of an inner power that makes the whole person receptive and obedient to a new way of living and serving in God's kingdom. This new way of living and serving has everything to do with the following elements of Christian living:

1. *Worship.* The act of worship becomes more than an inner attitude or private act. It is transformed from a spectator activity into a participation in the body of Christ, with everyone getting in touch with his position and function in relationship to others. The actor is Christ and not the pastor or some other designated leader or prompter. The power for unity and service comes from the dynamic presence of the Spirit of God, not from physical gyrations or manipulative monologues of a single leader. Worshiping God becomes a participatory holiness rather than an exercise of traditionalized or "canned" rituals. It is a coming together of all parts (members) of the body to celebrate unity of placeness and purpose. To depart from such an assembly without a renewed or recharged sense of fellowship in ministry under Christ is to fail in what worship offers.

2. *The Bible.* When the gifts are manifested among the faithful participants in the body of Christ, the Bible becomes more than a sacred, paper shrine to be visited now and then; it is transformed into a revered study source for holy and holistic living. The Bible takes on a new authority, not as a source of unquestioned doctrines, but as a holy corrective for human error related to apathy and false enthusiasm. It is interesting to see how those who have discovered their gift declare a renewed appreciation for and devotion to Scripture. They want to be scriptural in their understanding of God's grace and their special grace-gift so as not to abuse or neglect the use of it.

3. *Prayer.* Another of the spiritual manifestations is the new attraction and depth of prayer. This is especially true of praise and thanksgiving in prayer. Many have testified to a release from predominantly asking God for things, to praise and thanksgiving. They see so many more things related to them and their gifts that much of their praying becomes an act of acknowledgment and thanksgiving. This "charismatic" (giftedness) nature of prayer is such that it

saturates everything with which a person is involved.

Praying, therefore, becomes more than a formalized ritual; it is a constant awareness of and a new openness to God that make possible an active communion with him at all times. Even ritual and form in praying take on a new meaning. An example of this is the posture of bowing and rising. Kneeling symbolizes death or planting a seed; and rising with head up and arms stretched above symbolizes the blossoming of a new life.

4. *Witnessing.* Spiritual manifestations of this new life will also include the joy of giving witness to the presence of something beyond what the natural physical and emotional powers have to offer. This is not the classical "button-holing-people-for-Christ" activity, but a careful and deliberate attempt to be open to the direction of the Spirit and sensitive to the needs of other persons. The psycho-spiritual value of discovering one's gift and being willing to practice it for the common good of the body of Christ is that a person soon learns that witnessing is not just done with words. Persons with the gifts of service, administration, helps, hospitality, leadership, giving, faith, or mercy discover that the validity of such gifts does not reside in speaking, but in doing. The foundation of witnessing is love (*agape*) and love is something you do.

5. *Power.* I cannot close this section on manifestations of the spiritual source of gifts without saying something about the power of the spiritual presence of God (or Christ, or the Holy Spirit) that causes a person to be all that he can be. Human nature, regardless of the efforts we put forth to purify and perfect it, is under a curse beyond human control. Paul called it "principalities and powers," meaning evil forces. But the manifest presence of the Spirit or "spirituals" (1 Cor. 12:1) in the new life of a Christian brings a power (*dunamis*) to overcome certain aspects of the evil forces. God has gifted the members of the body of Christ

with certain abilities. These abilities, or charismata, counteract the evil powers which threaten to destroy all good. But the power that resides in each gift, apart from the whole, is not enough to repel the corresponding evil force. With all members realizing and using their gifts for the common good, no powers of evil or "gates of hell" can prevail against the whole body's force for good (Matt. 16:18). Evil's power can triumph only when Christians ignore or refuse to use their spiritual gifts for the upbuilding of the church.

In summary, the source of spiritual gifts is God who creates a special relationship with the faithful disciples of Christ who willingly form and participate in the body of Christ. This special relationship and gifts are for the sake of producing the "common good." Each person is not only one member of the body and thus a participant in the common good through his gift; he is also a member of the larger body of Christians everywhere as all embrace him for mutual righteousness. The link in these relationships is the Holy Spirit, the expression of God who brings together the dynamics of power, solidarity, enthusiasm, and productivity.

3

What the Spiritual Gifts Are Not

I REALIZE that a negative approach is not the better way of introducing most things. However, it is important for us to set aside some misunderstandings about gifts as soon as possible. The principle here is that it is just as important for us to know what some things are not as it is to know what they are.

Marriage offers a good illustration of this. I have been a husband for thirty-seven years. During that time I have learned the value of knowing what my wife does not like as well as knowing what she does like. It is no pleasurable thing, mind you, to hear her criticisms. But I have learned that if I want a meaningful and harmonious relationship with her, I'd better know what is her perception of a good marriage.

It has proven to be of inestimable value to know what not to expect or do as a Christian, if one is serious about a meaningful and productive relationship to Christ and his church. In order for this to be applied to our study of spiritual gifts and to build a basis for the value of the biblical teaching on gifts, we need to clarify what they are *not*.

Spiritual Gifts Are Not Acquired Skills or Natural Talents

A biblical truth and theological principle which is irrefutable is that all of life is a gift from God and all of life must be lived in a grateful response to God's ever-flowing grace. All the great teachers of the Christian faith have been saying this for centuries—and we believe it.

But what we are studying as spiritual gifts, charismata, is something in addition to the general gift of life. The spiritual gift is a new dimension to life that is known and experienced beyond natural man: " 'What no eye has seen, nor ear heard, nor the heart of man conceived, what God has prepared for those who love him,' God has revealed to us through the spirit" (1 Cor. 2:9, 10). This new dimension goes beyond anything that is a gift *from* God to that which is the gift *of* God, the spiritual gift being a mere manifestation of God's gift of himself: "To each is given the manifestation of the Spirit for the common good" (1 Cor. 12:7). Earlier, in 1 Corinthians 2:12, Paul says, "Now we have received not the spirit of the world, but the Spirit which is from God, that we might understand the gifts bestowed on us by God." Gifts, therefore, cannot be received or comprehended apart from God who is the giver.

If we are considering a natural ability or developed skill, to be certain, non-Christians and even atheists could outdo many Christians on any level. I have traveled throughout the Soviet Union and other Communist bloc countries, and have had ample opportunity to debate with Communists about the ideological and philosophical differences between the religious and nonreligious styles of serving mankind. I must confess that any one of those communistic atheists could put many Christians to shame in dedication, hope for mankind, and abilities, to say nothing of their vision and compassion. But we are not talking about such human attributes and achievements.

The fact is that much of what the church does is in trouble because we have relied on talents and training to do ministries for which we have no spiritual affinity. There is a difference between a talent or skill and a spiritual gift. The gift has a spiritual dimension that must not be overlooked. Simply because a person has an "appearance" or demonstrates an unusual physical or mental adroitness does not mean that he or she is endowed with the spiritual dynamic necessary for building up the body of Christ.

So often, perhaps more often than not, pastors and other local church leaders search for persons who possess special training or display special expertise to fill positions of ministry in the church. Rarely, if ever, do they give any consideration to spiritual affinities, calling of God, or spiritual gifts. On the surface, it would appear here that to suggest any other way of choosing people for service would be "organizational insanity." But the point is that the church in general and most congregations in particular are organized without regard to an understanding of spiritual gifts for ministry. And we are in trouble!

We search out and find persons who work as professionals in finances to be administrators of the local church's money matters. We delight in the discovery of a prospective member who is a public school teacher because most of the time we need Sunday school teachers. We find a man with manual skills that are used in his daily vocation and appoint him to do menial services around the church grounds and buildings. In all this we attempt to relate persons to positions in the local church according to natural abilities, acquired skills, and occupations—but at the cost of genuineness and effectiveness! And we wonder why so many of these burn out and the church grows stale.

Paul clearly offers an alternative to this. In 1 Corinthians 12:7–11 he explains that God gives the gifts for service in the body of Christ according to his will, not according to some selective process that takes into account only natural abilities and training.

This is not to suggest that God does not use natural abilities and training. To the contrary, often the talent or training is a vehicle or door through which the spiritual gift (charism) is made manifest. And it is extremely important for us to see the difference between the talent or skill, and the gift.

We often think of the person standing in front of a classroom as a teacher. We are conditioned here by the model of secular education. It may be, however, that that person in front of a group is doing something other than transmitting or communicating information. He or she may be encouraging, helping, counseling, or evangelizing rather than teaching. Yet, we call that person a teacher simply because he or she is filling a position. Many people shy away from teaching, or refuse to "teach," and rightly so, because they do not have the spiritual affinity for teaching. But they may respond positively to another approach that would not suggest the teacher-classroom-students model. Such a setting could be called a fellowship, or a sharing, witnessing, discipling, or Bible-reading group. Various spiritual gifts could be employed in these settings, not just teaching.

One reason we have so many complaints about church school curriculum is that the materials have been developed on the basis of the teacher-training model without regard to the various ministries—other than teaching—which can be done in a group setting.

Another point here is related to the dramatic and devastating decline in church school enrollment and attendance. We shuttle persons into "classes" for learning experiences, but their needs may not necessarily be related to education at all. Rather, they may need to be pastored, encouraged, or counseled. So-called "teachers" whose gift is not teaching find teaching aids and materials foreign and unfulfilling.

And the class members who may not be there to be "educated" or trained, but "edified" in another way, are even more frustrated. The teacher is discouraged by the members' inattention to what he or she has prepared. And this reduces motivation to teach and to attend.

Paul tells us one of the gifts is teaching (Eph. 4:11) and we infer from this that there are those who need that gift's offering. However, other gifts are aimed at some other kind of ministering than teaching. We need to begin a serious effort toward matching these needs and offerings. While it may be argued that everyone is in need of being taught, we certainly ought not allow anyone to assume this ministry unless he knows and demonstrates the gift for teaching in his service to Christ.

God makes no mistake in his gifting and assignments. When a person is gifted by God to teach (*didaskalia*), those for whom or toward whom the gift is directed will learn, and the body is built up.

Spiritual Gifts Are Not Roles

While it is essential to understand the difference between a skill or natural ability and a gift, it is equally as urgent to distinguish between roles or offices and gifts.

For example, all of us are called to the ministry of witnessing. This is a general expectation laid on all Christians by Christ, ". . . and you shall be my witnesses . . ." (Acts 1:8). He was speaking to his disciples who would receive the power of the Holy Spirit, but I take it that His words cannot be limited to those immediate ones. He includes us all—". . . to the end of the earth," he said. Paul expounds on the necessity for witnessing so as to impart grace to others: "Let no evil talk come out of your mouths, but only such as is good for edifying, as fits the occasion, that it may impart grace to those who hear" (Eph. 4:29).

This, then, is the general witness for which all Christians are responsible—a role, if you will. However, on a different level there is a special, articulate gift given for the purpose of bringing others to conversion. I speak of the gift of the evangelist (Eph. 4:11). This is not a role. It is a specialized power of God that is energized in a few who, when they are faithful, are effective in bringing people to Christ for the gift of salvation. Witnessing, as mentioned earlier, and the verbal activity of the evangelist may sound and appear to be identical, but the difference is in the results.

One more example of the difference between role and gift can be seen in the matter of giving. Every member of the church has the responsibility of contributing money to the work of the kingdom. This is the teaching of tithing as a vital part of building up the church for ministries. But to some members is given the *gift* of giving (Rom. 12:8). No one is excused from giving on a general or tithing level (not even the widow in Mark 12:41–44); but some are assigned a special ability to make contributions beyond the ordinary level. These special and abundant contributions are blessed by God to an extent that it appears the more they give, the more they are able to give.

A couple in one church I pastored felt that they were motivated by God to supply a large amount of money to be used at the discretion of the pastor. They were not interested in what happened to the money, only that it be used for needy persons. They contributed heavily to many other churches and ministries, to virtually all the national television ministries, and to others who learned about them and sought their help. It was obvious that they were not in business to make money for themselves, but to have enough with which to respond to various needs. It was also very obvious that theirs was not a gift of administration, for they couldn't stand being involved with the details of distribution. One of them said to me when I sought advice,

"Pastor, don't worry us with such details. Our ministry is to provide you with funds to meet certain needs. If you don't know how to do this, we'll give the money to someone who can. When you need money, let us know." Theirs was the gift of liberality.

Spiritual Gifts Are Not Offices

In the earliest Christian communities it was evident that, without rank and status, certain leaders surfaced with abilities and insights Paul defined as being grace properties for edifying and building up the fellowship. No names were given these positions, since organization was not the purpose for their being, but rather fellowship and service in Christ.

The nearest Paul came to labeling these ministries was to call them "co-workers" and "laborers" (1 Cor. 16:16; 1 Thess. 5:12, 13). These were not official offices we know today as pastors, teachers, presbyters, deacons, elders, and bishops. Paul's "co-workers" and "fellow-laborers" were of a "charismatic" nature, that is, gifted and motivated by the Holy Spirit.

The offices we know today came after the apostles passed away and were established mainly for the purpose of carrying on the work the apostles had begun. These ministries that were initially inspired and empowered by God's grace soon became a community possession. Near the end of the first century they were institutionalized and, as it were, set in concrete for the next eighteen centuries. In all branches of the Christian church today, offices and orders of official and professional ministries abound. When any mention of these offices and orders is made, we can be assured that they are not the same as those Paul described, which were initiated and maintained by the Holy Spirit.

It is enlightening and shocking to most ministers today to suggest that there is a difference between their office and the biblical notion of charism. So many of them have completely given themselves over to the notion that the church, as an institution, possesses and dispenses the gifts for ministry according to finely tuned and honed procedures for processing and ordaining.

We have a problem here. We all know ordained and certified leaders whose personalities, abilities, and effectiveness cannot truthfully be described as manifestations of the Holy Spirit, of which Paul speaks in 1 Corinthians 12. We all know teachers, presbyters, deacons, pastors, bishops, leaders, and administrators whose lives do not exemplify a state of being "in Christ" or, for that matter, "for" Christ. And at the same time, we know others who do not hold any official office or certification as ministers, but who have unquestionable spiritual power in their caring and serving as Christians.

A study of church history reveals much confusion about ministries as well as a profusion of uncertainties about orders. It is difficult for me to believe these had much to do with God, especially in light of the injunctions by Paul: ". . . I bid every one among you not to think of himself more highly than he ought to think . . . love one another with brotherly affection: outdo one another in showing honor . . . never be conceited . . ." (Rom. 12) and "Do nothing from selfishness or conceit, but in humility *count others better than yourselves*" (Phil. 2:3, italics added).

It seems to me that it is essential for us to restandardize ministries by the example of our Lord to be lived out in unselfish dedication, compassion, and spiritually directed service. We do not have to disassemble our institutionally designed and established orders and offices to do this. These can be vehicles by and through which the specific charismata may be directed for the common good of the church. The important point here is to know the difference between God's gifting and man's ordering.

Spiritual Gifts Are Not the Fruit of the Spirit

When I pass out questionnaires to ascertain the level of knowledge workshop participants have about gifts, the most common error (even among pastors) is mistaking the gifts for the fruit. When I went back to study great Christian thinkers and teachers of the past, I discovered the same misunderstandings. Augustine, Calvin, Luther, and to some extent, John Wesley—to name only a few—showed confusion in this area.

The fruit of the Spirit are found in Galatians 5:22, 23. In general, they are "love, joy, peace, patience, kindness, goodness, faithfulness, gentleness, self-control." These are not the same as the gifts, but, to be sure, they are connected in a very definite way.

"Fruit," a word that is singular in Greek, is often described as the first one of the list: love. Because of the richness of that word in Greek—agape—especially Paul's use of it, and because of its profound ramifications for Christians with reference to spiritual gifts, we are compelled to attempt to bring the two words together here. Mainly, I want to reflect upon the differences.

Without question, the subsequent attributes or virtues after the mention of love in Galatians 5:22, such as "joy, peace, patience, kindness, goodness, faithfulness, gentleness, and self-control," all issue out of the "more excellent" fruit, love. One could go further and suggest that the eight others are seeds of love which, when practiced or planted, sprout up as the real and abiding fruit of love. Paul's treatment of love in the context of explaining spiritual gifts is similar. He points to the "more excellent way" of love to which all other gifts point. His message in 1 Corinthians 13 is that without love all other virtues (fruit) and works (gifts) are considered nothing.

The fruit is what you *are*. A Christian has no choice in the matter of bearing the fruit of the Spirit. It is the nature of a Christian to be loving, joyful, peaceful, kind, good, faithful, gentle, and to have self-control. If he isn't, he'd better get on his knees and find out what has gone wrong. This *is* the test—fruit-bearing!

But a Christian does have a choice in the operation of the gifts. It is up to him to receive and manifest the gift(s). If it is refused, the power to be what God designed is lost, too. What good is a fig tree that bears no figs? Any other tree can serve as a shade from the sun or wind, but only a fig tree is natured and equipped to bear figs. If the gifts of the Spirit do not issue out of the nature and equipment to bear fruit, love, what good is your being a Christian? Others, even non-Christians, could probably do anything as well as you. While the fruit and gifts are related, they are not the same thing.

Spiritual Gifts Are Not for Self-glory

Paul addressed the noble subject of spiritual gifts amidst a climate of anarchy and conflict. It is obvious what he was up against. Those who were endowed with special abilities to minister began to elevate themselves and the importance of their gifts over other persons and their gifts. Members of the Corinthian congregation drew invidious distinctions between themselves and others, claiming pre-eminence for their particular gifts.

Paul sought to resolve this conflict by setting the gifts within their proper context. To encourage the expression of the gifts, he attempted to join or correlate the unity all of them had in the Holy Spirit with the unity they all had in the body of Christ. It was good, he said, for them to be exuberant over being favored by God, but spiritual pride had almost destroyed their witness to the lordship of Christ (1 Cor. 12:1–3). Spiritual pride had become the worst enemy of the church.

Paul's counsel has not always been heeded. Beginning with the Montanists in the first century, certain ones in the church have been all too ready to lord it over others through the prideful misuse of gifts they considered to be preeminent. This pattern has cropped up from time to time among Montanists, Enthusiasts, Pietists, Pentecostals, and mid-twentieth-century charismatics. Pride in believing what one has is superior to what others have has served as a ready wedge to create bleeding rifts between Christians.

This has occurred particularly with speaking in tongues (*glōssa*), divine healing (*iama*), prophecy (*propheteia*), and discerning of spirits (*diakrisis*). Extreme and bizarre claims have been made with the practice of these gifts, and at the expense of the essential accompaniment of the fruit of the Spirit. Consequently, two camps have formed: the "charisphobics" and the "charismanics," both hurling accusations at each other, misunderstanding one another, and confusing the silent majority in between. One wonders which sin is greater—gift-pride, looking down on others who don't possess certain gifts, or gift-denial, not believing in the existence of any gift.

Paul lays out a heavy message. The gifts are not for selfish reasons or self-aggrandizement, he says, but for the common good of the whole church, the building up of the body of

Christ, and the edification of believers. Pride or self-glory can never accomplish any of this.

Spiritual Gifts Are Not Divisive

There has been much strife and conflict over the gifts. Most of us know of fits of anger and even congregational splits over claims, uses, denials, and abuses of the same. This is so sad and unfortunate.

Throughout our history, Christians have been divided over too much or too little devotion to a good thing. In either case, the good, holy, and true will of God became the sacrificial victim. When such happens, we dare not blame it on the Spirit of God. God unites. Evil divides. It is not the will of God that separations occur on the basis of hatred or aggressive disregard.

When a congregation becomes divided over the use of spiritual gifts, someone has sinned. It is not the nature of the Holy Spirit to injure the body of Christ in any way. In fact, the nature and operations of the Holy Spirit are always to bring about unity, oneness in purpose, singleness of goal—the common good. The edification of the church is the strategic test of the authenticity of each gift. The importance here is placed on the health and wholeness of the body. An unhealthy body cannot produce the fruits of the kingdom. Only a healthy body can reveal what is righteous and holy. Our Lord preached this message as recorded in Matthew 7:15–20:

"Beware of false prophets, who come to you in sheep's clothing but inwardly are ravenous wolves. You will know them by their fruits. Are grapes gathered from thorns, or figs from thistles? So, every sound tree bears good fruit, but the bad tree bears evil fruit. A sound tree cannot bear evil fruit, nor can a

bad tree bear good fruit. Every tree that does not bear good
fruit is cut down and thrown into the fire. Thus you will know
them by their fruits."

Spiritual Gifts Are Not the Same for Everyone

In all the biblical passages dealing with spiritual gifts there
is no hint whatsoever of any one person having all of them
or of any one gift that is for every person. Furthermore,
there is no way to read the passages and be motivated to
"do your own thing."

While the gifts are given to individuals, it is in community
and for the common good of the whole body of Christ that
they flourish with legitimacy and effectiveness. Paul, in
1 Corinthians 12, uses the multiformity of members
(organs and limbs) of the human body to describe the
fact that we, as Christians making up Christ's body, are
different: "To one is given . . . to another . . . to another
. . . to another . . . ." This is to say, the gifts are for every
member of the body; but no member has them all. Paul
illustrates this by saying that the hand has certain characteristics which are *for* the whole body and not just the
hand, and that no other member of the body has the same
characteristics.

To accept the gifts that the Spirit bestows is not to commit
oneself to becoming a photocopy of every other "Spirit-
filled Christian." No, God respects our individuality and
personhood. If we were to survey the experiences individuals have in the Holy Spirit, we would discover that their
behavior, dress, and speech are not altered and molded into
one uniform "spiritual" kind; the personality and spirit of
a person are not eliminated.

The only legitimate conformity related to spiritual gifts
is openness and obedience to the Giver of gifts, never in

the practice of them. The only uniformity worthy of acceptance is to be in common subjection to the same Spirit, the same Lord, and the same God. When this is uppermost in our thinking and acting, the varieties of gifts, the varieties of service, and the varieties of results (1 Cor. 12:4–6) will be joyous occasions to celebrate God in all things.

4

What the Spiritual Gifts Are

IT IS NOW NECESSARY to give some attention to the positive characteristics of the gifts. We have seen what they are not; let's look at what they are.

Spiritual Gifts Are Unmerited Favors from God

The rich word *grace* is God's unmerited love poured out according to his own desire and will (1 Cor. 12:4–7). God's grace is essential for our salvation, our wholeness. This is basic for all who accept Christ as Savior and Lord. But the gifts, or as I call them, "grace-gifts," are special and diverse ones which God bestows upon various members of the church not only for the building up of the body but also for the fulfillment of the wholeness of each gifted member. While the saving grace is for everyone, grace-gifts differ from one person to the next.

The similarity in all of the gifts is that God makes the choice as to whom a gift is given; no amount of worthiness on the part of anyone can recommend him for the gift. A gift cannot be earned. It is something freely given and freely received, and God is the Giver.

The psychological and social blessings that accompany God's apportionment or assigning of the gifts are twofold: 1) The recipient is so pleased over his own gift or gifts and is so grateful to be divinely chosen, that he is motivated to do all he can with his gift(s) to express his gratitude in faithful obedience to God. 2) In fulfilling his own gift's potential, he never sees himself in competition with other members of the body. He finds himself delivered from envy or jealousy toward the giftedness of another. "Love is not jealous or boastful; it is not arrogant or rude. Love does not insist on its own way; it is not irritable or resentful" (1 Cor. 13:4, 5).

Spiritual Gifts Are Job Descriptions for Ministries

In our fallen and sinful condition, we could never design an effective redemptive force for our salvation. If what God has designed and given to the church has not met the salvation needs of the world, it is because the church has resisted, refused, and abused its role and responsibilities. One wonders what would really happen in our chaotic world if the church, as the incarnate body of Christ, became fully responsive to God's design and purpose for it!

Nevertheless, God's Word plainly tells what needs to be done within the church for it to be effective in its mission to the world. The spiritual gifts are the functional requisites for a fully operational force for salvation. The big question is why we are so ignorant of Paul's revealed secret and mystery of charismata for ministries.

Most denominations are having a rough time maintaining themselves these days. And most are in a battle against being "tossed to and fro and carried about with every wind of doctrine" as they try desperately to stay afloat. Many of them have enjoyed a long history of growth in adherents and influence, but this has now changed. They are declining in membership and influence for good. One wonders when the leaders will come to realize that it isn't being fundamental or liberal, theological or philosophical, radical or conservative that will cure the current chaos in Christian institutionalism, but that God has given us the answer.

God's design for health, vigor, unity, purpose, and productivity is the every-member ministry based on gifts given "for the equipment of the saints, for the work of ministry, for building up the body of Christ" (Eph. 4:12). The church, fallen into rough waters and being beaten hard by the winds of false confidence in tradition and programs, would do well to rediscover the New Testament model for choosing its ministers. It is sad to observe how some denominations recruit, train, and ordain people who do not know what gifts God has given for ministries; and many of these neither have a calling nor divine equipment. The only way out of this is to return to the basic acceptance of God's choices and designs. Understanding God's gifts and accepting what he has apportioned and bestowed as gifts for ministry are our only hopes.

Spiritual Gifts Are Aids in Discovering God's Will

Paul sets the purpose for being open to receive grace-gifts as a means of discovering and proving "what is the will of God, what is good and acceptable and perfect" (Rom. 12:2). I cannot think of a more joyous and meaningful life than one lived by the knowledge of and in dedication to God's will. Paul became so carried away with the thoughts of knowing and living by God's will for his life that he turned in his writing of Romans from a heavy discourse on Israel's history to a doxological celebration: "O the depth of the riches and wisdom and knowledge of God! How unsearchable are his judgments and how inscrutable his ways! 'For who has known the mind of the Lord,' . . . For from him and through him and to him are all things. To him be glory forever. Amen" (Rom. 11:33, 36).

Paul then ushers his readers into the privilege of making every sacrifice to know the mind and will of God. Nothing has given Christians more pleasure than discovering God's will for them. I cannot think of many things that have been more confusing and disheartening than attempting to function in a ministry to which one has not been called and for which he has not been equipped with the necessary gift or gifts.

Not to know God's will is to be as little "children, tossed to and fro and carried about with every wind of docrtrine, by the cunning of men, by their craftiness in deceitful wiles" (Eph. 4:14). To discover God's will is a liberating experience that brings new life and direction. This liberation also frees a person from the guilt of not doing or being unable to do something which God has never called and equipped him to do in the first place.

In the many workshops I have conducted I have seen a number of people liberated from guilt feelings upon discovering that their ministries and services had not been based on spiritual formations, but on social expectations. Pastors have been among these.

Many of these people carried guilt over their being unresponsive to requests for them to teach. They admitted that other services were far more appealing to them and that they would probably have responded favorably if asked to do them. But they were asked instead to take a class and that meant "teaching." Feeling uncertain and inadequate, they declined the challenge, but that left them with a load of guilt due to a "lack of dedication." Because of their guilt, they didn't feel good enough about themselves to volunteer for something else. When they discovered that they did not have the gift of teaching (Eph. 4:11), but some other gift, they were joyously released to explore other ministries for which they had a spiritual affinity.

I have seen pastors burst into sudden joy over discovering why they were "down" on themselves about certain ministries which they had been expected to do, but which were not consistent with their spiritual gifts. When they realized that certain chores were merely "roles" which had to be done because of the expectations of their employment or appointment, they could now zero in on their discovered gift(s) with greater energy and enthusiasm. They were not only delivered from guilt in not enjoying those roles; they also found themselves performing the roles with greater ease and less resistance.

Discovering God's will does not relieve a person from responsibilities in other areas of living and serving. But it will bring an abundance of energy to the exercise of his gift and to the other responsibilities he must carry out. Paul brings insight to this in Philippians 2:12, 13, saying ". . . work out your own salvation with fear and trembling; for God is at work in you, both to will and to work for his good pleasure." The gift is inside where God is. Working it out to various applications will of necessity be sifted through hard and unhandy things (roles and offices). But the joy comes in seeing the results of all things done in obedience.

Most, if not all, of us can identify things that bring no pleasure whatsoever, but which have to be done. The office of ordained and appointed ministry requires that some things be done that carry no immediate delight. Yet, the person who knows God's will and gift for his ministry will know that nothing is futile and senseless that pertains to the body of Christ. Some things may be more pleasurable, but all things are essential. To discover one's gift for ministry is also to discover God's will for unity and purpose in all forms of serving.

Spiritual Gifts Are a Guarantee of Effective Service

When you and I are sick or when age weakens us, it is rarely so because our whole body has become ill. All it takes is for one or two members of the body to stop functioning properly. This breakdown in communication between an organ and members of the body can seriously reduce the performance level of the entire body.

The same is true for the church, the body of Christ. When one or more members fails or doesn't know its function, the whole body is affected. Paul emphasizes this in Ephesians 4: ". . . each part is working properly, makes bodily growth and upbuilds itself in love" (v. 16b).

In the fall of 1982 I visited the Saint Paul Lutheran Church in Trenton, Michigan, a suburb of Detroit, to learn about this fast-growing church which had experienced astronomic growth in spiritual development and in its outreach in five years. The pastor, the Reverend Wayne Pohl, received my wife and me for an interview and there followed one of the most exciting discoveries of my life.

From 1977 to 1982 the church had grown from some 150 in Sunday school to 800, from a budget of around $150,000 to $800,000, from some 400 in divine worship to over 1,000, and in membership from around 1,000 to over 2,000. When I asked what happened, the pastor informed me that the church had established a policy and standard requiring all members to search, discover, and practice their spiritual gifts. At that time, more than 80 percent of those who were members in 1977 had gone through the spiritual gifts discovery program; 100 percent of all subsequent members had done the same.

"We have discovered where we belong in the body of

Christ," Pastor Pohl said. He then proceeded to describe the program by telling us what had occurred in his own life and how it had affected his style of ministry.

During the process, Pastor Pohl discovered that he did not have the gift of mercy (Rom. 12:8) which is necessary for effective ministry to those under stress or in distress. Until then he had wondered why he had approached hospital visitation with such negative feelings. (And with such a large membership, one can imagine how often he had to make hospital visits.) He was honest with his people and told them that he did not possess the necessary gift of the Spirit to be an effective servant during their illnesses. But he would continue visiting, and love doing so, if they so desired, he said.

The people confirmed him in his discovery and employed another staff member who did have the appropriate spiritual gift for effective ministry to the sick. This freed Pastor Pohl to give as much time as possible to the exercise of the gifts he did possess. Consequently, in five years he had not been back to the hospital to visit parishioners. However, consistent with his discovered gift of teaching, he had begun an adult Bible class which soon grew in attendance to two hundred every Sunday morning.

We can overlook the need to be effective by loading our pastors and members with other time- and energy-consuming ministries, but we do so at the expense of health and wholeness for the body of Christ. Wayne Pohl and his people decided that the whole body is too important for this spiritual truth to be neglected. Their philosophy of ministry is that every person has a gift and the church offers each a place for that ministry.

To be effective as a member of the body of Christ simply means that one must find his place to do God's will. God has gifted other members equally with placeness and power.

Effectiveness and growth come as the result of properly working together (Eph. 4:16).

Spiritual Gifts Are Means to Efficient Service

At the most, no local church can generally expect more than six to eight hours from any member during any week. It is only reasonable, therefore, to gain the greatest benefit from each member by utilizing the time available to the utmost. This can be done by helping persons serve where they are best suited. The discovered and acknowledged spiritual gift is the place to begin.

To be sure, someone will be quick to claim that although a person may not be physically present, he is nonetheless a bona fide member, and is working and doing his part. Granted! But the question still remains: what is being done while the body is not in assembly? Can you be a foot in one place (when the church is assembled with all the parts) and a kidney elsewhere? Can one be an "ear" in the congregation and a "liver" in the world? Too many people have tried to excuse themselves from an active and responsible participation in intimate relationships with other Christians, contending that they can be independent representatives of the gospel in the world "where it really counts"! This is a denial of the very nature of *ekklesia,* which means "people called of God." A Christian is called to be in community with other Christians—not with just another person in need, but within a fellowship of persons called into being by God. This fellowship requires identity and presence, as well as caring and sharing.

The church, therefore, is physical, spiritual, social, and psychological because it is made up of human beings who bear these characteristics. But it is more than a mere aggregate of such persons. Its fellowship (*koinonia*) includes an empowerment given by the Holy Spirit. This makes it to be more than any other human institution—a divine institution. While it does have an invisibility and hiddenness that defy logic, such a mystery must never detract from its visible and essential features of contact, unity, interdependence, and cohesiveness of purpose and direction.

A member of the body, furthermore, may apply himself in his trade or occupation in an honest and holy manner, but what he does may have little or nothing to do with his spiritual gift for the body. As does the physical body, the church has its basic unity in the physical, and this unity can only be fully realized in spatial and temporal relations.

Time and space, therefore, are important to the body of believers. And since few members have more than six to eight hours per week to give directly to the community and fellowship needs of the body, the development and use of spiritual gifts must be intentionally and primarily directed toward the body. To be sure, gifts may be used beyond and outside the fellowship and assembly of the church, but never without reference to the ministries of the body.

Spiritual Gifts Are Securities for Health and Growth

If we continue to utilize Paul's metaphor of human anatomy as being descriptive of the church, it would be reasonable to assign some expectations of health and growth to a local church whose members take gift-finding and use seriously.

The practice of medicine is predicated on a basic assumption about health, that is, health is important to a fulfilled life. Following that course, most health disciplines consider specializations necessary for artful therapy or healing, as well as for preventing illness. Each specialization was born out of the discovery of the essential value of each body part or organ for the good of the whole. The principle is that health depends upon the proper and balanced functioning of all organs and systems.

The health of a local church is no less important than the physical and spiritual health of each member. In fact, one of the spiritual gifts is healing (1 Cor. 12:9, 28). The gift (notice that this gift is in the plural) of healings covers physical, mental, social, financial, and spiritual health. I believe this is why it is in the plural form—there are so many ways health can be hindered and helped.

While, I am sure, other facets of health are not totally ignored in the healing ministries given to the church, I find more often than not a timidity, if not a silence altogether, regarding certain things. Requests for prayer are seldom heard for healing of mind, spirit, marriage, and social life.

In my visits from church to church for services of divine worship I observe that nearly all of the pastors write down the requests for prayer that are called out. Then they lift these up by name during the pastoral prayer. This is admirable. But what greatly concerns me is that nearly all requests are of a physical (health) nature. I have yet to hear someone call for prayer for healing between nations, peace for a troubled family or marriage, or a healing of some emotional illness. I have yet to hear someone call out a request for the healing of that church's effectiveness to minister to the mounting evils within the community or to pray for the loss of membership in the midst of a growing population—a population becoming more secular by the day.

A local church that discovers it is endowed with specialized gifts for ministry will discover that these gifts bring health and growth to itself. It will discover that health for the body, mind, and soul is essential for effective and productive functioning, and that wholeness and holiness are equated with health and growth.

Spiritual Gifts Are the Manifest Presence of Christ

Paul's analogy of the human body to describe the church physically is not the total picture. He speaks of God's Spirit residing in the individual member, which is to say, the very flesh and spirit of a person is the temple of God's dwelling. He would have us understand also that the corporate body, made up of several persons, is the scene where God is at work. The church is more than a mere aggregate of members. It is more than the sum of its parts. And what makes it more is the indwelling Christ who administers life-producing grace through the individuals to the whole body. The visible personality of the group becomes "Christian," that is, like Jesus Christ in behavior and mission (Eph. 4:11–16).

Spiritual Gifts Are a Guarantee of Lasting Results

Roles and offices for ministries in the church are significant, but are at best temporary and do not go far enough. Spiritual gifts, however, being from God as manifestations of the Holy Spirit, guarantee a permanent system for lasting results.

The results are "for building up the body of Christ" and are to provide opportunities for everyone to "grow up in every way into him who is the head, into Christ" (Eph. 4:12, 15). "To each," Paul said in 1 Corinthians 12, "is given the manifestation of the Spirit for the common good. . . ." "Strive to excel in building up the church," he said also (1 Cor. 14:12). The system for delivering such results is charismata, spiritual gifts.

The genius of Paul's use of the human body as a metaphor

to describe the church also suggests permanency. The members of the human body never get out of place. We can be comforted by the fact that when we get up in the morning we can expect the various parts of our body to be right where they were when we went to bed, and that their functions for the day will be the same as they were the day before. It would be a nightmarish existence not to know from one day to the next where the members, systems, and organs of one's human body will be!

One of the many joys of receiving God's gifts for ministry to and through the church is to discover one's peculiar gift and to live long enough to develop and use it as opportunities present themselves.

5

Varieties of Gifts, Services, and Results

IN 1 CORINTHIANS 12:4 PAUL says, "Now there are varieties of gifts, but the same Spirit; and there are varieties of service, but the same Lord; and there are varieties of working, but it is the same God who inspires them all in every one." This declaration forms the basis of our discussion in this chapter. It is the succinct, objective statement of what is found in the four main biblical passages having to do with the spiritual gifts—Romans 12:6–8; 1 Corinthians 12:8–11, 28; Ephesians 4:6–8, 11–14, and 1 Peter 4:10, 11.

The Romans passage lists seven gifts of the spirit: prophecy, service, teaching, exhortation, contributions, aid, and mercy. The Corinthian text lists seventeen: utterance of wisdom, utterance of knowledge, faith, healings, miracles, prophecy, ability to distinguish between spirits, tongues, interpretation of tongues, apostles, prophets, teachers, workers of miracles, healers, helpers, administrators, and speakers in various kinds of tongues. Ephesians enumerates five: apostles, prophets, evangelists, pastors, and teachers. And 1 Peter distinguishes two categories: whoever speaks, and whoever renders service.

When one subtracts the various gifts that are mentioned more than once, the total is twenty-one. But I do not think that such a list would encompass all of the gifts. Many, many more await to be discovered. To be sure, not everyone would agree with my position. I have read the literature on spiritual gifts and I can identify at least five different "schools of thought" on the subject.

One school says that there are no gifts today, that the charismata terminated with the passing of the Apostolic Age. The spiritual gifts, they say, were signs of the advent of the kingdom of God, nothing more—merely transient signs that pointed to the power and authority of the original apostles.

Then there are others who say that only certain gifts remain in operation today, and that the others ceased with the initial phase of establishing the church. This opinion claims that the so-called spectacular or sensational gifts—such as miracles, tongues, interpretation of tongues, and prophecy—were "sign gifts" and are no longer needed now that the church is established. However, other gifts that are needed for the maintenance and growth of the church are currently and powerfully operative.

Still others say that all the gifts are for all Christians, citing a portion of 1 Corinthians 12:6, ". . . it is the same God who inspires them all in every one." Such people claim that every Christian possesses all available gifts which may be used according to the demands of circumstances.

A fourth school claims that though they once belonged to individual members, the spiritual gifts have now passed on to and are in the possession of the offices of the church. Therefore, the church may dispatch or dispense with the operation of any or all gifts according to its corporate wisdom.

A different point of view says that the gifts are just as needed and valid today as they were in the first century.

People who believe this—and I count myself among them—
say that we see little evidence of the gifts only because of
ignorance (the same condition Paul met in 1 Cor. 12:1)
and disobedience (Paul warned against this in his letter
to the Thessalonians—1 Thess. 5:19).

I simply refuse to believe we know all there is to know
about God and that he has revealed all there is to know
about himself. I do not believe the Bible contains all God
has to reveal. I believe God is so limitless and all loving
that his future for us holds far more than we could ever
imagine (1 Cor. 2:9). I believe the future includes this
earthly life as well as life beyond the grave. John said that
there was so much more to what Jesus did that "the world
itself could not contain the books that would be written"
(21:25). If this was so then, how much more it would be
so today—after two thousand years!

This life—here and now, the life that is abundant (John
10:10)—is the life that we not only find *in Christ* as a
personal experience, but is also life in the body of Christ,
the church. It is a "body life" that is made up of an infinite
variety of grace-events or grace-gifts. Given to the individual
members of the body, these gifts make a sacrament of the
lives and services of those members. This is no less than
what we celebrate often in the sacrament of the Lord's Supper, or Holy Communion. We believe the elements, bread
and wine, are means of God's grace as well as symbols of
grace. Couldn't this also be applied to the body of Christ
whose members are favored and appointed by God for its
upbuilding? If the bread and wine are so sacred in their
symbolic value, how much more is each member of the
body of Christ as a "living sacrifice, holy and acceptable
to God"?

In the Lord's Supper we believe we encounter not simply
"tokens" or "reminders" of our Lord's broken body and
shed blood, but also our Lord's real and effective presence

within the community of faithful worshipers. Likewise, in the grace-gifts that constitute community—that is, people who have been chosen and endowed with spiritual abilities to edify the body—we encounter not merely persons of flesh and blood, but Christ himself, bestowing himself on the members in gifts he gives. Jesus Christ, the Giver and Gift!

If this is true, then we understand Paul's teachings about the varieties of gifts (1 Cor. 12:4). He was writing about the limitlessness of grace associated with the very presence of Christ in his own extended body, the church. And what we have here in 1 Corinthians is merely the tip of the iceberg. There is so much more to learn and to discover. But for a beginning we do have the listings. The very fact that Paul never seems to cover the ground the same way twice suggests strongly that the gifts he does list are more illustrative than comprehensive.

The central issue here is not the varying manifestations of the spiritual gifts, but rather that all gifts, ways of using them, and their results are of "the same Spirit . . . the same Lord . . . the same God." And who would dare limit God to twenty-one or two hundred and twenty-one specific manifestations of his presence and power? As I sit here and type, a heavy rain is falling outside and I am reminded of something Cyril of Jerusalem once said about the infinite variety of God's grace: "One and the same rain comes down upon all the earth, yet it becomes white in the lily, red in the rose, purple in violets and pansies, and different and various in all the several kinds." But it is the same rain. So, God's grace is the same, but the manifestations are obviously different. When we are tempted to celebrate certain manifestations as being more important or beautiful than others, we've lost sight of the giver. Without rain, there's no beauty in the lily; without the grace of God, there are no spiritual gifts.

Attempts at Classification

It may be reasonable to label some of the gifts as *speaking gifts*, such as exhortation (Rom. 12:8), utterance of wisdom, utterance of knowledge (1 Cor. 12:8), tongues, prophecy (1 Cor. 12:10) and teaching (1 Cor. 12:28).

Others may be classified as *serving gifts*—administration, helps, leadership (1 Cor. 12:28), giving, mercy (Rom. 12:8), and service (Rom. 12:7).

Sustaining gifts would include pastor (Eph. 4:11), apostle (1 Cor. 12:28; Eph. 4:11), evangelist (Eph. 4:11), and faith (1 Cor. 12:9).

A further classification would be *sign gifts:* healing (1 Cor. 12:9, 28), tongues (already listed), interpretations of tongues, miracles, and distinguishing between spirits (1 Cor. 12:10).

I have discovered in the available and popular literature, as well as by listening to tapes and hearing religious teachers on radio and television, such classifications are common; everyone seems to have his own scheme and virtually every teacher esteems some classification helpful. While there may be value in sorting out the gifts, the strongest word I should like to offer at this point is a caution against extremes. For example, in 1 Corinthians 12:8 the Greek word *logos* has been translated as "utterance" in some English versions and "word" in others. Based on one of these translations, using "utterance," some people list the wisdom and knowledge gifts as "speaking" gifts. Speaking gifts are audible ones. To utter something suggests, to them, an audible activity. What is obviously wrong with this is that they have overlooked the possibility of a better translation of *logos* into "word." And "word" can be a means of communicating something beyond merely speaking. The essence of Paul's use of *logos* here is communication, not a particular means or method.

Another caution should be noted regarding the "sign"

gifts. Some students of the Bible claim that the gifts of healings, miracles, and tongues were significant only during the formative period of the early church. Once the church was established, they contend, there was no need for extraordinary events to reveal the presence and power of God. Such a revelatory function of the gifts was transferred to the institutionalized church and its officials. The church became the incarnation of the power of Christ and therefore needed no unpredictable and extraordinary manifestations from individuals. God, they say, now works solely through the network of church offices and hierarchy.

This was an unfortunate, if not demonic, pattern for church structure that prevailed for centuries. It was demonic in that the laity became second-class citizens without rank and special graces of God. The upshot of this was that the gifts of the Spirit became the sole possession of a few. This is in direct conflict with the teaching of St. Paul.

There are too many dangers associated with systems of classification and dispensations. Either one can limit our hope of reviewing and renewing the claims of the Holy Spirit on the church in this new day of opportunities. Surely, there is much more we need to know about God and life under him. Perhaps, where we need to turn for another way of discovering God is to obedient service to him.

"Varieties of service, but the same Lord"

The Greek word for service is *diakonia,* a rich word that suggests a means by which one may execute the calling of God to declare and promote God's claim of righteousness upon the lives of others.

In the context of 1 Corinthians 12, the gifts (charismata) are given by the Spirit (v. 4) to service the means of salvation (wholeness and righteousness), simplified and exemplified in the life and teachings of Christ (v. 5), with the ultimate promise of bringing to reality the limitless works (*energe-*

mata) leading to God's glory in all things and persons (v. 6). What is striking about this passage that deals with service are the varieties (*diairesis*) of service, that is, the unlimited number of ways the gifts may be used. Unfortunately, in many denominations only certain persons may be designated as deacons, a word derived from *diakonia*. And the job descriptions often limit our understanding of the broader definition of ministries. Paul makes it clear that ministries or services known as *diakonia* are not designated persons or positions but rather acts by persons designed to profit or benefit the whole body.

The key word here is *diairesis* which means "many," "diverse," or "varieties." When this word is joined with the word *diakonia*, it becomes exciting to think how many ways the body of Christ may be ministered to and minister. For instance, take the gift of "utterance of knowledge." The many different ways of delivering or declaring a special message from God are staggering. Speaking with the mouth and writing with the pen are not the only ways. Messages from God may be acted out, painted, sculpted, woven, molded, carved, and sounded.

The gift of wisdom (*sophia*), a special truth or message (knowledge or *gnōsis*) from God, may be applied in such varied forms as ridding people of germs, creating safety, making laws, securing valuables, inventing and manufacturing means and items of health, educating, and doing a host of other things to secure opportunities for wholeness in worship, work, and play.

This application of the gift of wisdom makes room for services and vocations other than prayer, preaching, and playing the piano. It takes in plumbers, electricians, custodians, seamstresses, tailors, policemen, firemen, politicians, dentists, druggists, truck drivers—all who, in willing obedience, seek to provide for the welfare and building up of the body of Christ and not their own benefit and profit.

This is where we can bring together talents (natural abilities) and spiritual gifts. This is not to confuse the issue by equating the two, but to say that the spiritual gift of wisdom is manifested or acted out in and through the senses which also are required in the exercise of natural abilities. Take, for example, the wise saying, "Cleanliness is next to godliness." How can this be acted out in preaching, praying, or playing the piano? Not easily. But we can see very quickly that good plumbing, housekeeping, and medical practices can serve this bit of wisdom with satisfaction. Or, how can we take measures to purify or cleanse the blood of impurities that could cripple and kill if we don't use medical talents which require wisdom? In many cases we cannot pray, preach, or sing our diseases away. But the gift of wisdom can do this through applying skills of medicine, hygiene, and sanitation.

The different ways in which the varieties of gifts may be used in servicing the church for its growth and maturity are unlimited. Persons with the gift of leadership (Rom. 12:8) can fulfill their giftedness by dreaming up and creating more ways and means by which the other gifts may be used in servicing the whole body. Those with the gift of administration (1 Cor. 12:28), in turn, would find opportunity to exercise their gifts by implementing the direction and dreams of the leaders. In this way they would organize the body of Christ to receive the ministry of those who have the gifts of helps, teaching, and encouragement.

This process has no limitations. It could go on and on, attaining various levels of ministries and broadening scopes of services in a common pursuit of maturing "in Christ" (Eph. 4:13).

Varieties of Effective Results

One of the most encouraging aspects of the gospel is that we are never alone and that what we are called to do does not depend upon us alone. I have already said that we are called to be more than what we are and to do more than what we can. This is no riddle. It is a fact. On our own, in the flesh, we are hopeless. Who we are, without an identification with someone or something beyond ourselves, makes no sense. But because of what God has done for us in Christ, we can lift our eyes and hearts to new heights.

In the use of the spiritual gifts, we need only be obedient to see the results. And the results belong to the power of God. They are Spirit-empowered gifts which are capable of achieving powerful results impossible on the mere human level.

The word for this is *energematon*, a Greek word rich with meaning. It is one of the group of similar words from which is derived the English word *energy*. Paul is saying in 1 Corinthians 12:4 that the results have "varieties," that is, they are plentiful and different. Built into the definition of the Greek word is a power or effectiveness that is not merely a potential, but rather an actuality without limitation. What happens as a result of being obedient in the use of a gift in service to the body of Christ is more than the mere sum of the parts. The results are manifold and inestimable simply because they become the very energy of God flowing with purpose and freedom.

We do not have to worry about the results or operations of the gifts. This belongs to God. Our concern is to discover what gifts God has given us and to use them faithfully and in obedience. Nothing in the scheme of God's salvation is more demonstrative of his power than when man opens himself and receives God's gifts of grace. There is nothing that the church cannot accomplish for the good of humankind when it becomes receptive to God's grace. God has a design for every person and a plan for the whole world.

We do not have to worry about the welfare of persons, the needs of the world, and the future of the human family when we look to God and become what he wants us to be and to do what he wants us to do. To accomplish this, God has provided gifts, opportunities to use the gifts, and his own energizing power to make them effective.

6

The Gifts

Definitions and Behavioral Signs

A GENERAL DEFINITION of a spiritual gift is a special ability God gives to a member of the body of Christ for the specific purpose of building up the body for ministry to all other members and through those members to the world. This means that every member of the body of Christ has been given a special ability (or abilities). No member is left out of this scheme of God's operations. There are no spectators. And the ministry that each has is to the other members, and through them to the world at large.

With this general understanding of the gifts, I hope we can now proceed intelligently to comprehend what each gift brings as the "special ability" to the body. I will attempt to identify each gift, define it according to the Greek language, describe it in relationship to biblical contexts, and lift up some of the recognizable behavioral characteristics.

The order in which I list them is alphabetical, rather than the traditional classification method based on some hierarchy. Many authors see such a system in the mind of Paul, but I see something else in Paul's listing of the gifts. He begins by cautioning against thinking more highly of ourselves than we ought (Rom. 12:3), and in 1 Corinthians 12:22 and 23 he emphasizes the tremendous value of those parts of the body that appear weaker but are indispensable—the parts that are considered to be less honorable, but to which we accord greater honor. We need to keep this in mind when we run across his statements concerning "higher gifts." And we will want to ponder this when considering his list of God's first appointments in ministry as "first apostles, second prophets, third teachers, then workers of miracles. . . ." I don't believe he intended to set up a hierarchy of ministries, but was merely being numerically systematic as he called attention to the differing and varying gifts.

One of the great abuses of spiritual gifts is singling out one or more as the most desirable. This has caused much friction within the body of Christ. I will say more about this as we discuss the so-called "spectacular" gifts. If we keep in mind Paul's metaphor of the human body, we will be able to see that each member is a precious gift and is therefore significant. And with the psalmist we can say, "you created my inmost being; you knit me together in my mother's womb. I praise you because I am fearfully and wonderfully made . . ." (Ps. 139:13, 14 NIV).

The Gift of Administration

The Greek word *kubernesis* (coo-ber-nay-sis) is a word that often described the position and responsibility of the pilot or captain of a ship. Such a usage is found in Luke's description of the storm at sea (Acts 27:11). For our purposes, it appears in 1 Corinthians 12:28, in the list of gifts there, and is usually translated "administration." The gift is also implied in such passages as Acts 6:1–7 and Luke 14:28–30, the parable of the man building a tower.

This gift is the ability God has given a member of the body to match the gifts and talents of the other members to the purpose and goals that are consistent with God's plans.

The administrator is not the owner. He or she may not even be a visionary person, the dreamer, as is the case with the gift of leadership. The person who has the gift of administration (*kubernesis*) has the powerful ability to pursue the objectives laid out by the corporate wisdom of the body. He is not a dictator, nor does he administrate as one, but is firm in a conviction that "if you work the plan, the plan will work."

The person with this gift has an "organizational" mind, and is capable of putting things in order and perspective according to the prescribed plan; is quick to ascertain resources needed for accomplishing goals; and has an insatiable desire to know in clear detail what the goal or destination is. He has the ability to anticipate problems that may hinder and the needed talents to succeed.

This gifted person is prone to be conservative in handling resources in order not to exhaust the supply before completing the job. He doesn't always put his best or all of his available resources into action at first so as to hold some in reserve for a guaranteed finish. He often resists explaining why something is to be done and simply states what is to be done while organizing for results. Doing something, and doing it on schedule according to a set plan, is of utmost importance to him. He often appears to be "fussy" about details, but only because, unlike many others around him with other gifts, he sees the total picture and how all parts fit together.

A person with the gift of administration is often organization-centered, detail-focused, and time-oriented rather than person-centered. His joy is in smooth operations, forward movement, and not necessarily in reaching the goal. Once the goal is reached, he is often at odds with himself. He senses a need to get back into a process. In fact, this person, once the destination is in sight, begins looking for another project to be initiated as soon as possible.

St. Paul addressed himself to the neglects and abuses of spiritual gifts. There is such a thing as possessing a gift and abusing or misusing it. Abuse of this gift of administration could appear in a person's irritation toward others who may not understand the process. An administrator often gets the "big head," and the position causes him to "think of himself more highly than he ought" (Rom. 12:3). Or he may project his understanding on others and condemn them, causing them to feel guilty because they do not see what he sees. A person with this gift, who is acting outside the influence of the Holy Spirit, may use his position for personal gain. First Corinthians 13 is Paul's warning about how right things can be used in the wrong way and cause irreparable harm to the body of Christ. Love (*agape*) will not allow a person to seek a position of administration without the appropriate gift, and will not allow a person who has the gift to abuse it for personal gain.

The Gift of Apostle

The word comes from the Greek *apostolos* which means "ambassador, delegate, one sent out, a messenger, a herald." The word appears seventy-nine times in the New Testament, sixty-eight of them in Luke's and Paul's writings. The references to this as a spiritual gift are 1 Corinthians 12:28 and Ephesians 4:11.

An apostle, in a general sense, is a person who adheres to the personality and teaching of another and who willingly goes out to espouse the teaching and to placard the personality. An apostle, therefore, is an apostle of someone. He is not the message, but the messenger.

Much contention has been generated over whether or not we have apostles today and this comes from those who teach that the gift ceased with the passing of the Apostolic Age. Only the Twelve who were set apart by the Holy Spirit can be called apostles, according to this teaching. The remaining members of the body of Christ are disciples; none are apostles.

However, Paul became an apostle (Romans 1:1; 1 Cor. 9:1; 2 Cor. 12:12). Barnabas, like Paul, was not one of the original Twelve, but he was called an apostle. Other apostles are also named in the New Testament (see Acts 14:14; Romans 16:7; and 1 Thessalonians 2:6). The believers were warned against false apostles which leads us to believe there was no end to the giving of this gift in the New Testament period beyond the first Twelve. To be sure, there was no end to the need of special persons to be sent out as heralds and messengers of Christ.

Today's world calls for discipleship *and* apostleship as did the early church period. The apostle is the person who is given the special ability to move or go out to cultivate receptivity toward Christ and his offer of redemption. This ability may go beyond merely being a herald or messenger to that of effectively organizing and overseeing groupings of persons who are being discipled. Some people say that such persons are now called missionaries, but I believe this is in error and causes confusion. Missionaries are special persons with a special gift that takes them beyond familiar languages and cultures to minister in the name of Christ. Some missionaries may have the gift of apostleship, but not all missionaries are apostles; and all apostles are not missionaries. Some missionaries are not gifted as messengers or heralds, although they have gone out to fulfill Christian ministries in the fields of agriculture, medicine, education, or construction. They do not herald or proclaim the good news of Christ for the sake of winning people to Christ.

Rather, they act out Christian love in their professions. Their gift is something else, not *apostolos.*

It is important that we do not confuse this gift with an office in the church. The offices described in the New Testament are the elder, presbyter, bishop, and deacon. Apostle is nowhere included as an office in the church. Paul says this is one of the spiritual gifts; nowhere does he say that the *apostolos* can be transmitted from one to another by means of laying on hands and fulfilling ordination requirements. It is given by the choice and grace of God.

In our tradition, we have elevated the early disciples who were gifted by God with *apostolos* to a special place of authority and rank, and this has caused no little confusion. From this came the "apostolic succession," making all of the rest of the body of Christ "second-class" citizens. The New Testament does not support this medieval distortion of body membership.

Persons with the spiritual gift of apostleship will often be recognized for their ability and be put in denominationally established offices such as superintendents or bishops. But not all superintendents, bishops, and staff members have the gift of apostleship. This is evident from the decline of churches as well as ineffective ministries. But when the gifted person is matched with the position, the energizing Spirit of God makes evident the building up of the church, the honoring of Christ as the Head, and the winning of new disciples.

Discernment of Spirits

The Greek word for this gift, *diakrisis,* means to estimate, judge, separate, withdraw from, hesitate, discriminate, oppose, dispute, or to be free from doubt. When you look at all these references and attempt to put them into a meaningful statement to describe the gift, the definition comes out like this: the ability God gives to some members of the body of Christ to know with assurance whether certain behavior or teaching is of good or evil; whether of God, of Satan, or purely human nature; and to be able to use this information not as a matter of condemnation but rather for caution and health in the body of Christ.

The primary scriptural reference is 1 Corinthians 12:10, while Acts 5:1–11 certainly provides an instance in which it was necessary to discern the spirit. Several passages also serve to prove the necessity of such a gift: Matthew 7:15, 16:21–23; Mark 13:22, 23; 2 Peter 2:1–3, and 1 John 4:1–6.

Paul tells us that as Christians we are in a war. The battle we are fighting is not against "flesh and blood, but against the principalities, against the powers, against the world rulers of this present darkness, against the spiritual hosts of wickedness in the heavenly places" (Eph. 6:12). I know of no greater gift to aid us in this warfare than this gift of *diakrisis* or discernment. With so many doctrines and teachers and theologies and philosophies beckoning—along with so many crash diets of self-aggrandizement—it is no easy matter to know what is right and how to apply what is right in the right way. This gift brings us a hope for direction and health.

In the workshops I have conducted on spiritual gifts, I have met an unbelievable number of people who have discovered that this is their gift. It appears that God has blessed us with these persons. Perhaps it is time to find them and solicit their help. The unusual thing I have found is that no one particularly desires the gift; no one knows what it is. But when an inventory is administered, invariably several will score high on this gift. They are usually the first ones to ask for information about their gift because they are not sure what it is.

Typically, those who have this gift are not quick to judge behavior or programs. They are deliberate in order to "flesh out" what their deep feelings are. They tend not to seek after biblical quotations to firm up their feelings because they have prayerfully sought God's will. Prayerful reflection and spiritual intuition are paramount to this gift.

Persons with this gift often appear to be more concerned about what an individual thinks or does than about the person in question, and they can love that person sincerely while having grave reservations about his integrity. In this there is a discernment of what is possessing the person— good or bad forces.

These gifted people are often capable of seeing both sides clearly and taking a firm stand, and yet they may not be able to offer much of an explanation for their position. They see the issues with deep feelings, whether good or bad, right or wrong, without knowing why. They just know! When something is considered by them to be right or righteous, they feel elated and joyful; when something is not right, they are gloomy or depressed. And in both cases they may not be able to articulate why they feel the way they do.

Their decisions about issues and persons are often based on intuitive feelings rather than logic or scriptural references. Because of this, they are often accused of being emotional and illogical. But they "know that they know that they know." In meetings they listen intently and scan their feelings, rarely saying much in public simply because they fear they will be unable to explain what they discern. More often than not they are introvertive, perhaps bordering on being timid. It isn't popular to tell someone that he is not of God and is acting upon evil principles!

Making use of such people in the body of Christ is of inestimable value. I prefer not to ask them to explain *why* they see a thing as they do; rather I ask *what* they feel. In fact, I prefer asking such persons: "What do you feel about this project or issue or person? Good or bad?"

I have uncovered an interesting phenomenon. Most of

the wives of ordained ministers who have attended these workshops have discovered that they have the gift of discernment. Could it be that God, in calling these ministers, knew they needed this protection? I have noticed another thing: more women than men tend to have this gift and more laypeople than clergymen.

The application of this gift in the local church can help offset evil influences and enable the people to discover God's will. Surely God's will involves every person and every thing that touches the body of Christ. Nothing is outside his love. It is, therefore, conceivable that the enemy will invade the little and imperceptible things while the collective mind is being spent on "big and important" things. Enough of these small things can contaminate the whole. The gift of discernment can help flush out these unattended hindrances to perfecting God's will for the church.

Abuses, however, could abound in this ministry to the body. To be sure, Satan can counterfeit any good thing, and he does. It would be extremely important for the person with this gift to be much in prayer and meditation, and in touch with others who have the same gift. Praying for and with one another could go a long way toward eliminating possible abuses. We should never assume that because good persons are working that what they do will automatically be good. "Evil triumphs when good men do nothing," is a well-known warning. I would add to that: Evil triumphs when good men are not aware of the presence of evil. The gift of being able to see the evil as well as the good protects the body of Christ from being overcome by evil.

The Gift of Evangelist

The word *evangelist* comes from *euangelizo*, meaning to declare, announce, proclaim, or herald good news. Although it is used less than we would think in the New Testament, it is one of the richest words the Greeks had to express jubilation over some great gain. While it is used only three times in reference to persons (Acts 21:8, Eph. 4:11, and 2 Tim. 4:5), the word is related to the whole of the New Testament, namely, the good news of Jesus Christ who suffered death and was resurrected to procure for man the power to become whole (saved) in his relationship to God here and in eternity.

Obviously, some bearers of this good news are especially gifted to turn the hearts of their listeners or readers to the saving Christ. In Ephesians 4:11 Paul says that Christ gave "some evangelists." The gift, therefore, is a certain ability or power given to some members of the body of Christ who, when they willingly and obediently share their witness to Christ, see others moved to accept Christ as Savior.

In examining the effects of various gifts being practiced, it becomes obvious that some prepare the soil, others do the planting, still others water the seed, and the harvest is the pleasure of others (1 Cor. 3:5, 6). The evangelist is the one who effectively harvests the soul for Christ's offer of redemption.

The one with this gift of evangelism sees the harvest when it is ready to be reaped. He feels compelled to speak about his own experience with Christ, and is sensitive to the right timing of the spiritual harvest. He has a great admiration for others who are successful at winning people to Christ—who are reaping the harvest—and he studies their techniques.

His interest is mainly in the salvation of others, not merely their church affiliation, and he is more concerned about others' intimate experience with the living Christ than in their theology. He enjoys hearing about the conversion of others.

The evangelist's interest in other people's problems is

directly related to what Christ can do for them, not necessarily what they can do for Christ or the church. Often, when he reads or searches the Bible, it is not to prove that the Bible is true, but rather to use the Bible to reveal a person's need to know Christ. He enjoys a simple definition of religion and is not too fond of complex facets of theology.

Persons with this gift are usually the members most dedicated to the local church and have a higher record of attendance than others. They enjoy familiar music and hymns in the worship services, music with sounds and messages that move others toward a warm, vivid experience with Christ. During the sermon they find themselves praying for hearts to be touched and lives to be changed. They want the minister always to give an invitation after the sermon. If one of them preaches frequently he will almost always call for a commitment and a verdict from his hearers. If he is a layperson and the pastor and church do not offer opportunities for "souls to be saved" or brought to a definite commitment to Christ, he may want to go to another church where this is being emphasized.

The person gifted as evangelist often cannot understand why other Christians are not leading or attempting to lead others to Christ. He is more concerned about the sins of others and their deliverance than anything else. He or she tends not to be interested in social or economic or international issues except as these show the results of unforgiven sins and point to the need for Christ's redemption. He believes that relating persons to Christ would cure the world of all its ills.

The Gift of Exhortation

The Greek word for this gift is *paraklesis,* and is found in Romans 12:8. Jesus refers to the Holy Spirit as the *parakletos* in John 16:7, a word translated "Counselor" in many translations and "Comforter" in others. The meaning here is a ministry of standing by, sitting with, guiding, encouraging, strengthening, inspiring, giving instruction, consoling, aiding, and leading. This speaks of the Holy Spirit's function of leading people to a deeper knowledge of gospel truth, and transmitting divine strength that will enable fellow disciples to undergo hardships and remain true.

As a spiritual gift for ministry, it is the special ability a member of the body of Christ has been given in order to build up the body with presence, words, influence, encouragement, and motivating instruction.

The scriptural references are Acts 14:22, Romans 12:8, 1 Thessalonians 2:11, 1 Timothy 4:13, and Hebrews 10:25.

Since the Christian life is no easy way and since there are so many sources of discouragement, if not pain and failure, God has equipped the church with members who are powerful in their ministry of encouragement. It is amazing how a well-placed word and the right tone of voice can lift a depressed soul so that he or she soars with new vigor and direction.

I once knew a great Christian surgeon who was born and reared in China. One day when he was in a talkative mood he told me how he used to visit patients in a mission hospital with a minister. That minister would say to him, "Son, let's go see how many people we can heal with words today!" He had the gift of exhortation.

Everyone knows the power of a loving word, or a compassionate gesture; even the silent presence of a person communicates love in unspoken body language. While it is right to expect all members of the body of Christ to be encouragers, obviously some persons have special powers to heal, motivate, console, and inspire.

A study of these persons will reveal certain behavioral characteristics. They are often quick to speak a word of caution and instruction as well as comfort, but with a peculiar message of caring. These people are more concerned about the person or group to whom they are ministering than the project or event or issue involved. Person-oriented and feelings-centered, they know intuitively the value of emotions and how certain words and actions can elicit certain emotional responses. Unlike a teacher, their message comes from the experience of deep feelings rather than careful research or tradition.

The person with this gift has a keen desire to see the effects of following the guidance, instruction, and encouragement given. He or she believes in a process that may take time but that leads to fulfillment. This is why he sees value in sufferings and problems, as ways of learning and maturing. The urgency with which he gives advice may surprise others who will wonder at his being overly confident.

The person with this gift will often "jump in" and offer his own strength as healing and guidance. He tends to spend much time with those who are in need of encouragement or motivating instruction, but he or she will do so only so long as they manifest willingness and openness to change or to be helped. Many of these gifted persons find themselves going into the counseling profession. Those who become teachers or preachers develop a vocabulary filled with emotive words that inspire, motivate, and excite.

The Gift of Faith

This is where we run into some confusion. We almost have to go to the behavioral characteristics to see the real difference between general or saving faith and the special spiritual gift of faith for ministry.

The Greek word *pistis*, in reference to Christ, denotes a strong conviction about and dedication to the fact that Jesus Christ is the anointed one of God through whom we receive forgiveness for sins and, thus, eternal life. A person cannot be a Christian without this basic gift of faith. Simply put, the gift of faith is a special ability to use the power of general faith in order to appropriate a change or accomplish an objective in a particular situation, all for the good of the body.

The scriptural reference for the gift is 1 Corinthians 12:9, while Acts 11:22–24 serves as an illustration. There Barnabas is described as "full of the Holy Spirit and faith." Why *faith* here? Isn't it implied when a person is full of the Holy Spirit? Yes, but this was an extraordinary ability that Barnabas had. As a result a "large company" came to believe. He had the ability to extend the general gift of faith, appropriating God's power to accomplish what was good for building up the body of Christ.

Those who have this spiritual gift of faith for ministry are usually well-seasoned Christians who demonstrate their conviction. Theirs is a childlike faith; that is, they believe without questioning. They have a special sense or feeling about a thing that it is the will of God, and they speak more of God's will about certain issues, events, projects, or needs than calling for prayer or biblical proof that God wants it. Some may misunderstand them, thinking that they assert faith in such a way that prayer is discounted.

This faith is not always asking God for something. Often it is stubbornly believing God is going to do something even though the hours are long, the days are dark, and circumstances cry out to the contrary. In the process of their praying, however, they often have the experience of "praying through" on a matter. This means that after praying specifically for a matter, they reach the place where faith has done its work and now rests on God and his workings. No more prayer is needed. "It is finished."

These faith-gifted persons would rather believe something is going to be done by God than jump in and do God's work for him. We in the pastoral ministry know persons who demonstrate this. A professor of physics at the University of North Carolina, while I was his pastor, often displayed this gift. He would come in and say, "It's okay for you to go ahead with that project. It will be taken care of." I would often chide and ask, "Are you going to do it or have you lined up the support needed?" He would simply answer, "It's okay. God will see to it that it happens." And it did! He had "prayed through" and found God to be true.

These people of the special gift of faith do not go through all kinds of ritualistic acts to appropriate the results of faith. Their prayers do not have to be offered at an altar in a sanctuary or through special gestures. They simply and joyfully (which means without doubt) trust God for results. This faith, however, is not a cause for laziness or sloth. The persons so gifted are usually intentional and mature Christians.

The Gift of Giving

This gift, sometimes translated "generosity" or "liberality," comes from the Greek word *metadidōmi*, meaning to give over, to share, to transfer, to deliver from one's substance to the needs of another.

The basic scriptural reference is Romans 12:8, with numerous passages serving to illustrate a generosity in giving that transcends self to serve others. Selected passages are Luke 8:1–3; 21:1–4; Acts 4:32, 37; and 2 Corinthians 8:1–7.

While this is a basic standard of service for every Christian, there is evidence that God has given to certain persons an extraordinary sense of others' needs and the power to do something about it. The power, in many cases, demonstrates itself in the ability to acquire more and more resources out of which more and more substance is given.

The behavioral characteristics of this person so gifted with "spiritual" or "charismatic" generosity include not only the intense desire and motivation to give, but also special abilities and opportunities to give abundantly. This is often manifested in one's ability to make money and to have enough to give cheerfully. The giving is not with fanfare, but quietly, with a deep sense of satisfaction. When recognition is requested or accepted by the giving person, it is mainly to inspire and motivate others to do their share— whether or not they have the gift. The person with the charismatic liberality usually is alert to valid and worthy needs which may, in the ordinary course of events, be overlooked by others. He experiences joy when he learns that the substance he has given out of his gift answers a specific prayer and need. He is not stingy in giving, and ties no strings to the gifts of money unless there is perceived a possible abuse.

This person with the giving gift maintains a positive attitude toward the church's needs for financial assistance. He or she never sighs saying, "There they go again, and here I come again!" He or she rarely has any second thoughts about whether or not those receiving may be worthy as long as the body of Christ is aided. I think of a man who won $20,000 in a golf tournament and was immediately approached by a young and poor mother whose sick child needed an expensive operation. He felt so moved by her condition and the story of the child's illness that he gave her the check—$20,000! Afterward he was told that he had been "conned"—the woman had no child and she had done this to others. He replied with great interest; "You mean, you really mean that there is no child who is that ill and in need of expensive surgery?" "That's right," answered his informer. "This is the best news I've heard all day," said the gifted giver. "I am so thankful to God that there is no sick child."

In many cases, these gifted people are well off and they demonstrate unusual faith in and joy toward God, considering their opportunities to give a blessing. They are the givers who do not grumble when "expensive" ministry needs are explained. They tend to jump into any program that involves all members of the church; they enjoy being a part.

If they are in a right relationship to Christ, they do not brag about what they give, and they never criticize others who are not giving as they should or could. They are willing to maintain a lower standard of living in order to give more to the needs of the church. They never give any thought to "buying" attention from other church members or God by generous giving, nor do they attempt to dictate financial policies of the church. In fact, they often feel that they've not given what they want and need to give, although they have given extraordinarily, even sacrificially.

The word *haploteti* (translated "simplicity" in Romans 12:8) means self-abandonment, singleness of eye, or simple kindliness out of the sheer joy of giving. It often connotes sacrifice, but with a joy that can sustain and motivate further giving. In other words, it is not necessary for a person to be wealthy in order to give. The giving of the "widow's mites" was one of the greatest demonstrations of this charismatic generosity (Luke 21:2).

7

The Gifts

The Gift of Healing

THE NEW TESTAMENT Greek word for "healings" is *iamatōn*, a plural form, meaning "cures" or "healings" related to conditions that are consistent with God's will. The verb means to cure (or be cured), to make (or be made) whole—to be healed physically, mentally, emotionally, socially, morally, theologically, philosophically, and spiritually.

The scriptural references to *physical* healings are Luke 5:17, 6:19, and 9:2, 11; to the *mental*—Luke 9:42; to the *moral, theological,* and *philosophical*—Isaiah 6:10, Matthew 13:15, John 12:40, 1 Peter 2:24, James 5:16, and Hebrews 12:13; to *spiritual* healing—Luke 5:20.

This gift or gifts is the power God gives to certain members of the body of Christ either to serve as healers or channels of healing, or to receive healings from various kinds of illnesses that hinder and disrupt the body in its ministries. More will be said about those who serve as "channels of healing."

This, perhaps, has been the most abused of the charismatic powers. We all know about the abuses. I do not want to go into that. But I do want to deal with the scriptural idea, the biblical fact, that indicates there's more to it than healing from cancer or some other frightening physical illness. I want to point out the behavioral characteristics of the authentic healers and the truly healed.

The charismatic healer is quick to discern any unhealthy condition that hinders the progress and wholeness of the body of Christ, not merely the condition of one person. He often sees a condition as an opportunity for God to bring the individual and/or the body of believers back to himself. Such a person will pray only for the will of God in the matter.

Often he appears to be more concerned about illness than health, and he is, in fact, if the body of Christ is being hindered. Because of this, he tends to overlook the *person* while concentrating on the *condition* of illness. He doesn't always know or claim to know the results of the use of his gift. He will not publicly reveal the contents of letters from those who extol his healing gift. In fact, the authentic healer is not interested in trying to "prove" his case.

This person will often be misunderstood as he explains that the condition for which healing is requested may be God's appointed process toward a greater wholeness (such as a person's attitude and outlook) rather than a mere healing of the specific hurt or pain. Often, the charismatic healer has a gift-mix of exhortation (encouragement), discerning of spirits, knowledge, and faith. He is not usually, if ever, found holding "healing crusades" with fanfare and personalized billing. He or she is found mainly to be operative within the body of Christ, and for specific purposes related to the healing of persons being hindered in their ministries.

The authentic charismatic healer does not have a need to mimic or copy stock phrases, gestures, and words—"In the name of Jeeeeeeeessuss, come out! I command you to

be heeeeeeeeaaaled!" Often, however, a quiet and meditative laying on of hands, with no word spoken, is the manner.
The authentic healer does not tend to separate healing of
the body from the total context of Christian living. He or
she readily sees emotional, moral, attitudinal, doctrinal, and
social ramifications of evil or illness that need the wholeness
only God can provide. He often hurts deeply inside when
too much emphasis is put on physical illnesses, knowing
full well that many requests for healing are self-centered
and hedonistic—for the avoidance of pain or displeasure
and the desire for pleasure.

The authentic charismatic healer often wonders why the
pastor or others in charge of ministries in the church do
not lift up the healing aspects of God's grace. He is often
attracted to other healers, but feels very uncomfortable over
the way they either present themselves or practice their
gift of healing. This gifted person is attracted to the healing
stories of Jesus and others so gifted in the Bible. The healer
is often moved with intense compassion when confronted
with a condition of illness in others, and wonders immediately why God has not done something about it. When
hearing of a healing that is assumed to be a direct result
of God's gift of healing, the healer does not react with suspicion but rather is jubilant and gives thanks to God.

The healer is often critical of those who claim to have
been healed but are not intimately and serviceably related
to or involved in the church's active ministries. The authentic charismatic healer does not claim that all illness is of
the "enemy" and, therefore, not the pleasure or will of
God. He or she is realistic about the limitations of life,
even as a Christian. This healer sees suffering as a means
of healing—a healing of a condition that goes beyond physical health.

I want to say a brief word about the recipient of cures
or healings, those "channels" of healing—persons through

whom God works in a healing way, a person or group who has been healed. (And I mean "healed" in all its senses here.) Certain characteristics are prominent. "Charismatic" recipients of healing have a deep sense of need to be at their best in ministry to the body. Their request for healing does not come out of a simple, selfish desire to be well, but rather in order to be functional in a responsible ministry for the upbuilding of the body of Christ. These people do not tend to think only of physical illnesses that hinder ministries, but have a concern that covers a wide spread of ill conditions. Thus they encourage the attitude that expresses gratitude to God for allowing a healing as a means of influencing others to turn to God. The charismatic recipient of healing will not mind being a vehicle or means of communicating a message to others even though it may mean his or her temporary lack of wholeness.

Please note that most of these characteristics are not typical of the healers and healings that have become commercialized and popularized. Charismatic healings are for the edification of the body of Christ, not for the popularity and selfish interests of the healer or the healed.

The Gift of Helps

On the surface, the Greek word *antilepsis*, found in 1 Corinthians 12:28, means "to aid and assist another in need." A deeper understanding of this word can be determined from a Greek noun: *antilambanomai* which describes the acceptance between a person being helped and another person giving the help. This implies not an objective, passive association between the giver and receiver, but a deeper reciprocal relationship. The "receiver" offers himself as does the giver in the same opportunity to minister. The stem of the word *lambano* describes receiving something through the senses, an active and lively experience.

This gift is the ability not only to aid or assist objectively a person in need, but also to be mutually benefited (built up or edified) by the needy person in what he brings to the relationship, thus fulfilling both needs of giving and receiving.

The word *antilepsis* appears only one time in the New Testament, in 1 Corinthians 12:28, but many illustrations of this mutuality between giver and receiver can be found. Some are Romans 16:1, 2; Acts 9:36; Luke 8:2, 3; and Psalm 21:1. In the last reference a reciprocation between giver and receiver can be seen. The psalmist cries: "In thy strength, O Lord; and in thy help, how greatly he exults. . . ." While God gave him all the desires of his heart, the king found himself with the greatest blessing of all: ". . . glad in the joy of thy presence." With this gift of helps, the giver is grateful for the opportunity to serve in God's name, and he finds blessings and fulfillment in helping another. In like manner, the receiver feels fulfilled in something that extends beyond whatever he has received— the presence of God in the life of the giver.

The person with the gift of helps feels compelled to give from his talents to help another. He delights not so much in what he is helpfully doing as in the dynamics of the relationship between him and the helped. He rarely, if ever, questions the legitimacy of the needed aid. He sees the person in need not as an object of charity, but as a part of himself in the sense that they are together in the body of Christ. He feels as though he has done something for himself when he has done it for another. And the aid becomes a sacred system of communication between the helper and the one being served. What he does gives birth to warm feelings toward the one he has helped—not a sense of pride or importance (superiority). He gives aid not because he loves, but rather, to love. The recipient of his aid is made to feel, not an object of charity, but rather that he has been apprehended by a force greater than either or both—the presence of the living Christ: "I was hungry and you gave *me* food. I was thirsty and you gave *me* drink" (Matt. 25:35 italics added).

The Gift of Hospitality

Some students of the grace-gifts do not include this in their list of charismata. I do because it is evident that some people are especially blessed by God with the unreserved willingness and ability to attract strangers and make them feel wanted, accepted, "at home." I must also point out that most references to "hospitality" (*philoxenos*) in the New Testament appear to cover a general standard of behavior for all the members of the body of Christ. However, from my own research and observations I have concluded that certain individuals become effective catalysts; they minister in such a warm and friendly way that the body opens up to receive strangers with warmth and love.

The word *philonexia* means "love or fondness of strangers," and it comes from two Greek words: *philos*, meaning friendliness, accepting, and openness; and *xenos*, meaning stranger, alien or outsider.

Animals and human beings are "territorial" creatures. And this is true not only in a geographic sense. It includes ideas, rituals, and groupings based on similar affinities. Primitive man's basic unit was the family and whatever associated with that. This was not to be invaded without extreme challenges and counter-challenges. Anyone outside of the household was a stranger and unwanted. Boundaries were rigid and sacred. This aspect of man's nature manifests itself in all types of fraternities, guilds, clubs, classes, tribes, cults, and religions. Christianity was to be different. It was founded on the "great commission" to evangelize *all* peoples, *ta ethne.* This means freely and openly offering special, loving attention to aliens and strangers. While other cults and religions did not and could not reach out to outsiders, this was the genius of the Christian movement (John 3:16; Matt. 28:19, 20).

Certain persons were given a special grace (favor) of God to reach out and receive strangers openly and winsomely. The Bible demonstrates this. See 1 Peter 4:9, 10; Romans 12:13; 1 Timothy 3:2; and Titus 1:8.

The observable characteristics of those with the gift of hospitality, the special power to attract outsiders, are as follows: They delight in meeting new persons. In fact, it appears that they prefer to be with the uninitiated, the outsiders. They are quick to respond to the special needs of strangers for lodging, food, entertainment, and companionship. They do not hesitate to offer help to people who are in need.

The charismatically hospitable person tends to be "gushy" in approaching visitors, and may appear to "come on strong." This often is interpreted by those who do not have this gift as seeking personal approval from those who do not know the group. Nevertheless, the charismatic lover of visitors is more interested in doing whatever makes the visitors feel comfortable and fulfilled than in demonstrating talents for meeting those needs. He or she is person-centered and not program- or group-centered. When they converse with strangers, they usually center on interests related to the strangers' needs and desires rather than on what the program or group has in mind.

These charismatic outreachers may appear to be bored with or negligent of established friendships in their attempt to spend time and energy on "new" persons. They usually feel more comfortable in short-term relationships than in longstanding ones. Neatness of place (home) or excellence of program (church) are not prime considerations with them before they invite guests. They consider a new relationship with someone the most important transaction taking place—not the meal or bed in the home, nor the service or program in the church. This love of strangers often endures and delights in personal hardship in order to serve guests.

The difference between this person and the one who has the gift of evangelist is that the hospitality gift enables a person to see Christ in the stranger—"I was a stranger, and you took me in" (Matt. 25:35). The evangelist usually sees the stranger as one who needs to meet Christ or as one to whom Christ is taken through preaching and teaching (see Acts 8:26–40). This gifted person finds an affinity with Isaiah who heard the call of God, " 'Whom shall I send, and who will go for us?' " and replied, " 'Here I am! Send me.' " The call of God here was not to the person, but to a people; yet, a person (Isaiah) answered. This charismatic friend to strangers will quickly respond to any attempt by the church to reach out to the unchurched masses who are "sheep without a shepherd."

The Gift of Intercessory Prayer

The Greek word for this is *enteuxis* (ent-yook-sis), found in 1 Timothy 2:1 and 4:5. Other references to this type of ministry are in Colossians 1:9–12, Acts 12:12, and Luke 22:41–44. The word means a conference, a petition, a bringing together, to petition, or intervene on another's behalf.

The spiritual gift of intercession is the ability God has given to certain members to bring the other members and their needs before God for special consideration until there has been a satisfactory answer to the prayers.

These persons have a special ability to stay long with a petition until some evidence of answered prayer is manifested. They experience a special and somewhat inordinant amount of delight in praying for others. These are they who, in early periods of history, spent their lives in monasteries or convents; their total ministry was prayer. Today, these charismatic intercessors are eager to fulfill the requests of others for prayer.

I have heard that some twenty thousand such prayers assemble each morning at daybreak in Korea and that they always include America in their specific petitions. When I heard that they sometimes are very sad upon coming to the "Prayer Mountain" and not finding a single request from the United States, I sat down and typed a whole page of requests and sent it to them. They were grateful and told me so.

Unique characteristics of persons so gifted are the flashes of insight and urgent feelings they have about certain people, urgent feelings related to prayer. They find themselves praying on behalf of people whom they have not seen or thought of in years. Also, they frequently feel an intense "burden" to pray for someone or something. Once they are in prayer a flash of insight—the thought or image of a person—comes to them. Later, they often find out that the person whose image appeared to them was in need, right at that moment. While this may be the experience on occasion for nearly all Christians, it appears to be a rather common occurrence for persons who have the gift.

Some of these prayer-gifted persons claim to have a "prayer language" that facilitates their praying (see 1 Cor. 14:2). Many of them say that the language unknown to them helps them in their intercessory praying because they do not know why or for what they are praying; they only know that they are prompted to pray. They say that they mentally concentrate on the person or situation and let their speaking mechanisms run freely.

Those with the gift of prayer usually respond quickly and definitely when their pastor or other worship leader announces special prayer requests. They are inclined to call the pastor and ask for more details, not that they are "nosey," but they want to pray specifically and effectively. They consider prayer a vital ministry and not simply idle words or nods in God's direction. To them it is work—a meaningful, joyful work—designed to accomplish something. They do not delight so much in bringing God to act upon the needs of others, as they do in bringing others and their needs into the presence of God and maintaining that presence until the people are changed or their needs are met. This is the hard work of it—not fainting or giving up (Luke 18:1).

One more characteristic of this gift and the obedient use of it should be mentioned. I used to hear the term "praying through" when I was young. People would occasionally testify to "praying through" on a matter. In my workshops on the spiritual gifts I have asked if anyone had experienced such a thing, and I can only recall a half-dozen persons who have claimed such. However, when I delved deeper with those who have the gift of intercession, I found that while they may not have used the term, they know what I mean and indeed had experienced "praying through." It is the sense that all is well, that their work is now done, of being relieved of the pressure of praying further, of being free to move on to something else. These same people told me that in such instances their prayers were answered in some definite way.

The Gift of Knowledge

The Greek word for this is *gnōsis* (no-sis) and characterizes a gift that imputes to a person a special insight and understanding of God and his will concerning the church and its ministry. This is not a knowledge in the sense of acquired data. It is a specific grasp of certain information that is unlike (in content and source) that which is referred to as "natural" or "worldly." Such knowledge may pertain to this world and the "natural" order of things, but it has a special bias and source related to God. While every person who has committed himself to Christ and, thus, has received the Holy Spirit, has a dynamic source of understanding spiritual things beyond any natural understanding (1 Cor. 1, 2), to some God has given a gift of advanced understanding. This gifted person has a special ability to bridge the distance between the biblical Word of God and God's current Word for modern man. Often, this special understanding of God's current Word may transcend the Bible and its contents, that is, its culture, places, language, idioms, geography, data, and events. But it will never conflict with the Bible in ultimate meaning and reality.

The scriptural references are found in Romans 11:33, 1 Corinthians 12:8, 2 Corinthians 11:6, Ephesians 3:19, and Colossians 2:3.

Knowledge is the ability God gives to certain members of the body to understand the eternal, timeless principles of God that can produce righteousness and productivity for man, especially in relationship to the church and its discipling all peoples for God's kingdom.

The one who has the charisma, the gift, of knowledge knows deeply that he knows that he knows. He tends to be theological in his analysis of situations. By "theological" I mean intelligent thinking about God-man relations. He is often viewed by his peers as being mystical or spiritual with regard to life and living. He tends to be meditative rather than talkative or active, and he seldom gets riled. He is firm and confident in what he says. Speaking out of his gift, he doesn't need the expressed approval of people to whom and for whom he speaks. He is speaking God's truth—who gives him the only approval he needs.

When he speaks from what "he knows that he knows that he knows," he may appear dogmatic and highly opinionated. His insights often reach beyond exact quotations from the Bible to moral and social principles based on the eternal concepts of love and servanthood, not laws. He has the ability to distinguish between what is culturally derived and what are eternal, universal principles. Meanings and overtones are of greater importance than gathered facts and data. Doctrines that are founded on principles rather than on words and events are of great interest to him.

A theologian I know said of the book of Revelation, "The book simply but profoundly means, 'Hang in there. Don't give up. All of this has meaning. It will soon be clear to you and worth it all.' " With those few words he captured the meaning of that difficult book. This is typical of those with the gift of knowledge. They are not always able to see the practical application of the principles, being more "theoretical" than practical.

The Gift of Leadership

The word "rule" or "lead" comes from the Greek verb *proistemi* (pro-iss-tay-mee) and is one that often described the position of a seaman who stood on the bow, in front of the others, to point out the destination and ways and means of reaching the port. He was not the owner of the ship, but one who set directions and inspired others to follow.

The scriptural references to this as a spiritual gift are Romans 12:8; 1 Timothy 3:4; 5:17; Titus 3:8, 14, and Hebrews 13:17. I define this as the ability to set goals for the body of Christ, to see what is essential for the well-being of all involved, and to motivate others in such a way that the body will enjoy harmony and accomplish its objectives.

The characteristic qualities of those who have this gift are as follow: He or she tends to see goals and individuals as directly related; they see how the individuals concerned

personally benefit in the process toward and the attaining
of goals or dreams. This is why we are drawn to a person
with this gift—he or she does not lose sight of the value
and needs of the individual in the process toward goal-attain-
ment. The gifted leader usually finds himself "out front,"
pointing out ways that appear impossible, but in an inspiring, positive, fresh, and challenging manner. He is quick
and firm in pointing out obstacles in the way of progress
for individuals and the whole body. He will often attempt
to explain to us the importance of the forward movement.
He is a dreamer, a visionary with goals of great accomplish-
ment for the body.

This person demonstrates a great personal need to estab-
lish long-range goals, some of which may be beyond the
comprehension of other members of the body. In such cases,
he will say, with a special degree of confidence in his ministry, "Just trust me. It's okay. You'll see what I'm talking
about as we move along the way." And people follow!

He has a great ability to keep those goals in focus even
as he cultivates the fellowship of individuals along the way.
He demonstrates a special understanding of group dynamics,
although he may be untrained in such, and develops methods of good communication and group harmony on the
basis of the value and need of every individual.

In his or her use of biblical literature, this person tends
to grasp and be more concerned with broad principles found
in the Bible than specific rules, laws, and commands. He
sees love as stronger than law, harmony more important
than doctrine, and faithful service more important than
rituals in corporate worship. His understanding of theology
and doctrine tends to focus on function rather than form,
on meaning rather than systems. To him the ultimate realities of the faith are directly related to inner or intimate
reality, that is, a personal experience with Christ that serves
as a prologue for kingdom living and the eventual consum-

mation of all things. This is why he is gifted in relating individuals to one another, as well as to himself, without losing sight of specific and future goals.

He is considered to be an example to follow rather than the best follower. He is quick to volunteer to lead a project even though he may not know what the project is at first. Confident in his ability to lead others to whatever the goal is, he is often thought of as conceited or egocentric, even manipulative, because he finds ways of being in leadership positions. He may appear to be more visionary than practical, more futuristic than contemporary. He has a great amount of tolerance, even in the presence of those who disagree with him or with whom he disagrees; and he tends to view criticism as a source of benefit, not a challenge.

Having a wide grasp and understanding—even an appreciation—of different responses by others, he sees these with a positive value. He does not hold himself aloof from his followers, but tends to develop close relations with them. He never develops a following based on rank for himself or on criticism of the inferior qualities of others; rather, he does so by warmth and friendliness. He places great value on his being honest and having integrity in all that he does and is careful to follow his own advice. The key thought in all that he does is trustworthiness. He wants to be trusted because he views his goals as being trustworthy, as being God-given and worthy to be attained.

The Gift of Mercy

The spiritual and grace gift of mercy comes from the Greek word *eleeō*, (el-eh-eh-o) and means more than simply doing something for or extending help to a person in distress. It is actually experiencing the pain of the other person. It is a feeling with and for a person in misery in such a way that an act must follow which relieves both the person in distress and the one doing the act of mercy. *Eleeō* is the same word that describes God's mercy for the undeserving, mercy that caused him to be ". . . in Christ, reconciling the world to himself" (2 Cor. 5:19).

Scriptural references to this special quality given to certain persons for Christian living are Matthew 20:29–34; Mark 9:41; Luke 10:33–35; Acts 11:28–30; 16:33, 34; and Romans 12:8.

Mercy, as a gift, is the special ability God gives to some members of the body of Christ to feel genuine empathy for others who suffer distressing physical, mental, or emotional problems; and to translate that feeling into cheerful acts that reflect Christ's compassion to and through the body of Christ.

The mercy-gifted person actually feels the pain or misery of another. He or she has no inclination to administer hurt or pain, even in the process of helping, and if pain is involved in the helping, this person will apologize profusely. He has the tendency to respond quickly to any form of suffering—emotional or physical. The *el* prefix of the Greek word means "delight" or "excited," and the *eeo* means "acts"; thus, the person delights in or is excited about helping to free another of misery.

This person often appears to be a "bleeding heart." He may become victimized by those in misery who use their condition to manipulate others for attention. However, such a person, with the gift of mercy, possesses an unusual ability to detect insincere motives or false misery and can withdraw from it immediately. He never considers the worthiness of the person in real distress; and he tends to be more interested in unhealthy or distressed people than healthy ones. He is condition-oriented rather than person-oriented; that is, he is attracted to the sickness, pain, or suffering more than to the person who suffers. Relieving the condition also releases the gifted person from the suffering he feels.

This gifted one often feels inclined to look for those in need or distress if none is readily at hand. A severe abuse of this gift ought to be mentioned. When a person is not acting in Christ with his gift of mercy, when there is no one around in need of help and the gifted person cannot find anyone, he or she may create a problem in order to be on hand to give help. Many people play this game of "enemy-then-savior" out of a misuse of the gift. All gifts have their misuses and abuses, as well as counterfeits.

The person with the gift of mercy is often what we consider "emotional," easily given to expressing sympathy by groaning or crying when confronted with another in pain. Persons with this gift can be easily identified if you watch television dramas with them. The misery portrayed on the screen will affect them visibily. When they hear stories of sorrow and suffering from the pulpit, they are quick to rally to any attempt to relieve the misery. Because they want to know when the distress is relieved, many of them enter professions that are directly related to the relief of suffering. Their delight is in relieving and being relieved of pain. In this respect, then, what happens between the helped and the helper is not merely a transfer of aid from one person to another in need, but a mutual fulfillment and enrichment of the participants in the exchange.

8

The Gifts

The Gift of Pastor

THE GREEK WORD for "pastor," *poimen*, (poi-mayn) means "shepherd." The chief scriptural references are Ephesians 4:11; John 10:1–8; Acts 20:28–31; 1 Timothy 3:1–7; and 1 Peter 5:1–5. The word means to protect, to oversee, to care for, to manage, to assemble, to feed. These can be taken literally or figuratively. It is a concept heavily used in the Old and New Testaments, and a very important one.

This is not one of the offices for ministry we find in the New Testament, such as deacon, elder, presbyter, and bishop. It is a gift for ministry that anyone is eligible to receive. While persons in certain offices we normally associate with ministry may be given this gift of pastoring, the gift itself is certainly not restricted to those offices.

The behavioral characteristics of the gift of pastor would, no doubt, be akin to the responsibilities of a herdsman (Old Testament) or a shepherd (New Testament). A pastor would be one able to carry a concern for a large group of members of the body of Christ. We could define the spiritual gift as the ability God has given to various members of the body of Christ to oversee, care for, and spiritually develop a large group of members, especially over a long period of time.

This person has the drive and capacity to shoulder concern for many people at one time. He tends to be concerned about spiritual and physical needs that relate to maturation and participation in the body of Christ. He is quick to respond to a call for help, but also seeks to get others involved in the helping. Having a keen awareness of healthy and enhancing relations between people, he is often paternalistic and nurturing in his relationships. He knows that problems are going to occur and plans ahead how these may be solved. If problems do not come to his attention, he tends to go looking for them. He experiences a joy in the management of ministries for a group of people and prefers group dynamics and programs over a one-to-one ministry. He easily spots "bellwether" people (sheep) who can aid him in the ministries and he innately understands that, like sheep, many of the members will follow others more quickly than they will the appointed leader.

The one who has the gift of pastor can easily identify with the problems of others and can bring to bear upon those problems the Good News of Christ, the Good Shepherd. He always knows that he, in reality, is an "undershepherd" of Christ (1 Peter 5:4). In preaching or teaching, he tends to lift up the gospel values that relate to peace, harmony, cohesion, unity, purpose, common goals, and fellowship, the principle being, "united we stand; divided we fall." He tends to be group-oriented rather than person-centered.

When approaching a strayed member, he is likely to think and say, "We have been missing you," or "What can we do to bring you back to us?" He has a keen sense about group dynamics and how individuals best relate to what the group has to offer. Counting members does not offend him. This way he can keep track of possible losses, a thing shepherds fear greatly. He is also expressively concerned about growth or maturation. Physical and relational growth are indicators of his performance quality, something he takes seriously.

I have noticed that many church school teachers do not have the gift of teaching (more about this later), but do have the gift of pastoring. It would be far better for us to help them understand that what God has placed them there to do as pastors is far more important for the edification of the whole church than transferring biblical information to the members. It is a mistake to design and to develop teaching materials based on secular standards of teaching excellence and turn such over to those who are gifted to pastor, and not to teach. We need to design material that would help people pastor, if that is their gift. Does anyone ever imagine a shepherd teaching a flock? No, but we do vividly imagine such a one caring, encouraging, relating to, managing, and feeding.

There is, however, a related gift of teaching (Eph. 4:10). What if a person has both it and the pastoral gift? Those with the gift of pastoring, and not teaching, but who find themselves in charge of a class on Sunday mornings, spend more time during the week calling, caring, and visiting their class members than they do in preparing lessons. But those with the gift of teaching and not pastoring, may spend all their time preparing the lesson, never making contacts with their class members. This is also characteristic of ordained ministers. Those who have the gift of pastoring will spend most of their time in direct contact with programs and members while the ones with the gift of teaching will spend most of their time studying and preparing for their next (mostly corporate) contact with their parishioners in the classroom.

The Gift of Operations of Power (Miracles)

No particular Greek word can easily and indubitably be translated "miracles" in English. Yet, many translators do this with *dunamis* (see 1 Cor. 12:10, 28). Since, however, the words *dunamis, dunameis,* or *dunameon* are often translated "power" or "miracles" and since many of us shy away from the word because of certain abuses and connotations, my preference is to translate this "powerful works," from the combination of *energemata* (operations or workings) and *dunameon* (of powers) in 1 Corinthians 12:10. Whether we translate this as "miracles" or "powerful works," there it stands. And it is not beyond our ability to recognize those who have been used mightily by God to do things that go beyond even the gift of faith. Today's world needs some "powerful works" of the Spirit if we are to find meaning and purpose in the midst of so much chaos.

Scriptural references to such powerful operations are plentiful; a few of the most notable are 1 Corinthians 12:10, 28; Acts 3:1–10; 5:9–11, 12–16; 9:32–35; and 13:8–11. This gift is the ability of some members of the body of Christ to be used of God as special means of powerful works that transcend ordinary and natural methods and ways.

The behavioral characteristics resemble those of the gift of faith, but with a slight difference. The difference is in the lack of intentionality in the use of the gift. A person to whom God has given this power of operation or work does not necessarily know what is happening. He does what he is stirred by the Holy Spirit to do, and something happens.

Paul, in 1 Corinthians 12:6, says that there are varieties of workings (*energemata*) or results of the powerful energy of God. We do not know how and where or when these energies will flow, or how long it takes for a powerful thing to be accomplished, but history is full of such. This gift is unlike any other. Teachers know when they are teaching, hospitable persons know when they are loving toward strangers, givers know when they are giving, leaders know when they are leading, and so on. But the person with the gift of powerful operations does not and cannot say, "Now I am going to perform a miracle! Get ready, now! Here it comes!" No, all such gifted persons express great surprise over the results of their faithfulness. Some have not lived to see the result of God's powerful working through them, but it happened. A good example is the first martyr, Stephen, and the miraculous (powerful operation) impact of his death upon Saul of Tarsus. The conversion of Saul was indeed a miracle, and so was Augustine's.

We could continue this with lives and events spreading over two thousand years, but it suffices to say, most of the great humanitarian movements and reforms, whether or not religious in motivation, were begun without a grandiose scheme for their future. Instead, as we look back now, we can see that God's power to accomplish good for mankind was obviously given to unsuspecting peoples. Such goes on today, "for the gifts and the call of God are irrevocable" (Rom. 11:29).

The Gift of Prophecy

The Greek word for this is *propheteia* (pro-fay-tee-ah) and indicates a discourse that is divinely inspired, a declaration of the purposes of God related to a current, concrete situation—whether by reproving and correcting the wicked or comforting and admonishing the afflicted. It is the telling forth or forth telling of a truth believed to be revealed by God for the present or future. The prophet is one who divulges, makes known, speaks out for, announces, instructs, comforts, confronts, encourages, rebukes, convicts, and stimulates people whom God has chosen to receive a special message.

The scriptural references, for our purposes here, are 1 Corinthians 12:10, 28; Ephesians 4:11–14; Acts 2:14–36; 15:32; 21:9–11; and Romans 12:6. The gift of prophecy is a special ability God gives some members of the body to receive and to communicate either longstanding or recently revealed truths and messages to God's chosen audiences for the purpose of building up the body and its ministries to and through itself to the world.

People with this gift are articulate. They are often capable of discerning the character and motives of people, and are able to identify evil or wrongs. They are willing to experience personal brokenness in order to understand and demonstrate the brokenness in others.

Paul illustrates this with his acceptance of suffering, hardship, and a "thorn" that caused him to experience the sufficient grace of God (2 Cor. 12:7–9). Suffering may not always be the result of evil, but rather a heavy gift of God (see 2 Cor. 4:7–12). Strongly dependent upon Scripture to validate their experiences of prophetic revelation, they tend to be frank, even caustic or tactless when they defend their statements. Often they have the experience of inner weeping as they identify personally with the sins and the evil of the world (see 2 Corinthians 11:16–30).

Normally they have a broad view of God's kingdom and righteousness, covering all of life, not just spiritual concerns. Their focus on rights and wrongs is often judged to be dogmatic and intolerant. Their emphasis is often on making decisions on the basis of what their audience already knows of God rather than the slow process of education and spiritual growth. Their bold, strict standards may hinder intimate and personal relationships. A strong sense of urgency impels them to call for a decision or response to their pronouncements; they are restless as long as decisions and responses are pending. They accept the press of deadlines and are comfortable with time-lines and tables, as well as revelations, found in the Bible. They often feel that play is unimportant, even wrong, until people receive and act upon God's revealed truths. A work-ethic is important to them. They are usually results-oriented rather than process-oriented.

The Gift of Service

The Greek word for "service" is *diakonia* (dee-ak-on-ee-ah) and connotes a special service to God done in a variety of ways; mainly it has to do with menial, ordinary tasks and their extraordinary results. All the scriptural references are too numerous to list, but these are representative: Romans 12:7; Acts 1:17, 25; 20:24; 21:19; 1 Corinthians 12:5; Ephesians 4:12; and 2 Timothy 4:5.

The word *diakonia* is used in a variety of circumstances and ways, and is often translated "ministry" as well as "service." An actual tracing of these uses will uncover its representation from the most menial and basic tasks of serving the needs of fellow humans to the high privilege of serving God directly through prayers of adoration, proclaiming good news about Christ, and priestly acts on behalf of others.

While it is a fact that the term *ministry* later became descriptive of a class and rank of persons, the New Testament use of the term *diakonia* (ministry or service) did not intend anything that related to political or priestly services. The Greeks, during the time of Jesus, recognized it at once as pertaining to self-abasement—waiting tables, serving food and wine, cleaning up after a meal. This is what our Lord brought to the meaning of ministry (*diakonia*)—an honorable and loving service that could not do too much or stoop too low to show esteem for and to service the needs of other persons (see Matthew 4:11, Mark 1:31; Luke 10:40; 17:8; John 12:2, and Acts 6:1).

The word implies the essence of discipleship as being work and service for the benefit of others, never for holy rank (hierarchy) or status. Ministry, therefore, is not a status or position, but a loving act of caring for the needs of others, whatever those needs are.

The charismatic nature of service or ministry is revealed in the life and acts of a person when there is seemingly no limit to his ability and willingness to serve in the most humbling and inferior position or circumstance (Luke 22:26, 27); serve he must!

The man or woman with the gift of service is keenly alert to detect what needs to be done and is quick to act—never waiting for someone else to "show" first. He tends to feel and display a sense of joy in whatever service is undertaken—menial or profound. He tends not to care about or even notice how menial or unpopular the task or job is. It is a form of worship and ministry to him, regardless of what it is. He displays a physical stamina, almost beyond belief, to fulfill the needs that must be met. He doesn't usually hesitate to use personal funds to get the work done, so strong is his desire to complete the job. To leave a work undone for God would be missing the mark, a sin.

Some precautions need to be mentioned with regard to the person who serves. This person is likely to go overboard or become too involved in many projects because of the delight and joy he derives from serving. Too, his quick response to service may prompt suspicion of self-advancement and, thus, jealousy from others. For his part, he must beware of being critical of those who do not share his motivation and interest in the task. His insistence on serving rather than on being served may appear as a form of rejection of others' attempts to express the same gift. And if he senses insincerity—a "put-up-with-the-job" attitude among his fellow workers—this can create tension.

The essence of the gift is not law or power, not position or status, not rank or authority, not dignity or esteem, but service to the body of Christ. The variety within this one charisma is as wide and numerous as are the needs within the body. When we lay the emphasis on the body of Christ, we guard ourselves against the danger of fanaticism that comes from charisma without some form of institution; and at the same time, when we stress the importance of ministry or service as being a free-grace gift, we shore up against the other danger of being hollow or "white-washed sepulchers," having the institution without the charisma.

The Gift of Teacher

The Greek term for this is *didaskalia* (dee-dahs-kal-ee-ah) and is a rich word meaning to teach or instruct concerning the things of God and man's necessary response to God, especially under the influence and power of the Holy Spirit (1 Cor. 12:28; Eph. 4:11; Acts 13:1; and James 3:1). This is the extraordinary ability God gives to certain members of the body to expound and make simple God's offer of redemption through Christ and his will for righteous living.

This does not necessarily mean that the person who has the gift of teaching has the gifts of knowledge and prophecy, although, in many respects and applications, they are similar. It does mean, however, that the gift of teaching will carry a special power to elucidate and illuminate, to clarify and simplify, and to illustrate the role of Jesus Christ as representative of God in man's redemption. It may be that the charismatic teacher, gifted by God, finds it absolutely necessary to rely on other gifted persons for information, revelations, and divine disclosures. But he can do so with the added extraordinary ability to use what he receives from them with edifying results, not only for others but also for himself (Heb. 5:12; James 3:1).

Much is being said and written today about Christian education. A multitude of institutions are devoted to teaching the Bible, religion, church history, doctrine, and theology. Because this is true, I have a deep concern that we recognize a growing problem.

There is no question about it—the early Christians slipped quickly into and became obsessed with a teaching ministry that was based on secular models. The charismatic model or mode of teaching ministry was almost, if not totally, abandoned. The pastoral Epistles reveal how quickly and how far the early church moved away from the reliance upon the Holy Spirit for instruction, correction, and sustenance, as Paul insisted and maintained to the end. This has continued throughout history, even to the present.

It grieves me to learn how many seminarians become disenchanted upon discovering that the seminary is not a community of faith but that it is seemingly obsessed with maintaining academic integrity as one department competes with other departments, all at the costly expense of offering the students little or no spiritual formation and development. Most students who survive with a sense of the "Holy Other" (a sensitivity to the presence of the Holy Spirit) are those who serve student pastorates where practical and spiritual problems constantly drive them to their knees before God for strength and guidance. Seminarians who are not blessed with the practicum of the parish while being educated tend to model their ministry after the classroom professor and wonder why the community of faith does not respond as the early New Testament peoples did to the prophets and teachers!

An associated problem is our method of training leaders and teachers in the local church. In all too many cases, no attempt is made to ensure that those we recruit and train for leadership are experienced Christians—"born again" (John 3:3), "in Christ" (2 Cor. 5:17), "transformed" (Rom. 12:2). Even the literature we turn over to our local leaders bears little testimony to the importance of such experiences of faith. And we wonder why churches are declining in influence, why more people leave than are received as members, and why the church is accused of not offering the "real spiritual part of religion." Teaching is the key, but only a charismatic kind.

Charismatic teachers differ from those modeled after secular standards. While they place a premium on accuracy of details, the meaning of words and phrases, they radiate with an enthusiastic devotion to Christ as Lord and Savior. They delight in reading the Bible and discover the Bible to be full of relevant messages for today. They are more inclined to search out the *meaning* of Scripture than memorize verses, events, names, and titles of books. Yet, they consider memorization of verses, events, names, and book titles indispensable aids toward grasping the meaning.

These teachers, gifted with the Holy Spirit, will not overlook the hard work of being accurate in details, correct in the use of words, and ardent in research. Yet they will balance these with appropriate personal attention to other needs of the students. To them, teaching is more than the transmission or communication of information; it carries a relational feature. Teaching, to them, becomes more than a methodology, technique, or event; it is an identification and involvement with people who are in process toward a new being in Christ. They do not find it easy simply to "deliver" a lesson to those before them in a classroom situation while having no relations with them at other times. The charismatic quality of *didaskalia* creates the motivation to be in partnership with the learners. It is a mutually benefiting relationship that carries the principle: "teaching, I am taught."

In addition to being "relational" in their teaching roles, these gifted people also delight in researching meticulous details. They tend to verbalize their feelings as well as act them out; are keenly interested in validating new information by proven systems of verification; and they have an insatiable love for books, magazines, and other reading materials. Slow to abandon well-thought-out traditional views and ways which have been effective in building up the body of Christ, they will not accept so-called "propositional truths," "scriptural accuracies," and "doctrinal exactitudes" without empirical proofs with practical value for today's living. This simply means that charismatic teachers are not interested in sifting out historical facts and fiction, but rather in finding meaning and purpose for living. The better term to describe New Testament teaching is discipling (Matt. 28:19).

The Gift of Tongues

This spiritual gift is described by the word *glōssolalia* which combines two words: *lalia,* signifying any utterance of sound, whether intelligent or unintelligent, and *glōssa,* meaning literally "tongue," but implying "language." Glossalalia nowhere appears in the New Testament; usually the Greek word translated "tongue(s)," is *glōssa.*

Scriptural references are 1 Corinthians 12:10, 28; 13:1; 14:4, 5, 22; Mark 16:17; Acts 2:2–13; 10:44–46; and 19:1–7. Some Bible students also include Romans 8:26, 27 and Ephesians 6:18 as references to speaking in tongues.

Tongues is the special ability or power God gives to some members of the body to communicate in a way that may or may not resemble a known or acceptable language for the purpose of transcending the limitations of normal speech to minister to, for, and through the body of Christ.

To be sure, this has been one of the most troublesome

aspects of charismatism, beginning early in Christian history. I do not care to enter into the debate over the gift
of tongues. There are more books and pamphlets on the
subject than the human family deserves, and I do not intend
to add another one. We cannot, however, overlook the existence of this charism in the New Testament and its occurrence throughout history, especially since it seems that the
greatest volume of interest in the subject prevails today. I
simply want to point out what I have discovered as the
universal characteristics of those who believe in tongues,
even if they are not necessarily speakers, and of those who
speak in tongues in private prayer and/or in the assembly
(church).

These grace-gifted people have a very real and active
prayer life, which they rarely neglect. They are inclined
to pray aloud, usually beginning their prayers in their own
language and moving into sounds that free up the thoughts
bound by the limits of syntax and word definitions. They
have a keen inclination, even a conviction, that there is
much more to praying than saying the conditioned and
learned words and phrases. When they pray or speak or
sing in tongues, there is no stammering or sighing, neither
standardized exclamations of joy nor a mumbling of gibber-
ish. The flow is almost effortless. The genuine use of this
mode of speaking is personalistic and individualistic, not
copied from or set by the pattern of others. Those who
are true recipients of this gift do not go into a trance or
become delirious, and are not normally given to ecstasy
or highly emotional aberrations. They are never out of control of their senses and feelings nor do they feel "delivered"
into the control of the Holy Spirit. They are always in control of their participation.

They would not describe this as the Spirit praying or
speaking for or through them. Rather, to them this is the
awe-inspiring experience of having the ability to participate

fully "in the Spirit" so that a special ministry may be performed.

They do not always—perhaps rarely—know the content of what is being communicated, but they do know the joy of not being restricted by a learned language and thought pattern. They have a special sense of being in touch with God. Eventually these people discover a pattern of sounds which becomes for them a personal prayer language. Most of them so gifted are not particularly curious about what they are praying or saying—they simply feel a great sense of trust in the act of praying.

Many of those with this gift claim that when they initially experienced it, it was the most transforming and enlightening happening in their relationship to God. Eventually, however, as they matured, they became aware of the gift's being a pointer to and support of a more meaningful ministry. The gift has a twofold dimension: (1) to edify or build up the person with the gift so that (2) he or she may be inspired, directed, and strengthened to serve others effectively. Often, the gift when exercised gives a sense of direction and a release from unnecessary pressures. People feel lifted from a conditioned sense of low self-esteem to that of divinely inspired personal value and destiny. Many find deliverance from psychological and emotional problems, even to the extent of being healed of related physical illnesses, and some feel their sense of psychological balance restored so that they regain a confidence about what they can and cannot do.

In their relations with others, many find the gift an aid to loving. Their religious convictions are strengthened with its practice and their religious life is revitalized as a direct result of using the gift. They usually find that church services and the sacraments take on a new meaning, the Bible "comes to life," and prayer becomes more a means of relating than petitioning. Most of the faithful uses of this gift give witness to a particular quality and quantity of joy, even in the midst of difficulties.

As with all of the gifts, there is a danger of "gift-projection," that is, thinking and declaring that all Christians should have this one gift. Some recipients tend to make others feel inferior or disobedient if they do not have the gift. To be sure, some appear to be out of control in the use of the tongue gift though they claim that the Holy Spirit is doing the speaking. Nowhere in the New Testament does it say that the Holy Spirit does the speaking. In every case it says, "And *they* spoke in tongues."

Whenever tongues becomes divisive in the body of Christ, the burden rests on the practicer. All gifts are to edify, never to divide and tear down (Eph. 4:12–14). To pray to receive this gift is to abuse the gift. Charismata are free-favors given by God, from his own choosing. A charism sought after and petitioned for and earned through fervent prayers is no longer a free gift; it is no longer a charism.

This gift is abused when anyone thinks or promotes the idea that through it a possessor will acquire eternal bliss, whenever one uses it in public without an interpreter (1 Cor. 14:27, 28), whenever a person praying in public begins in his own tongue and then prays only in his personal prayer language (1 Cor. 14:15), whenever he believes and teaches that it is the panacea for all problems and the answer to all mysteries, and whenever he separates himself from those who do not have the gift or leaves a church because this gift is not being demonstrated publicly.

The Gift of Interpretation of Tongues

It is obviously essential that this gift be considered in relation to the preceding one. Without the presence of the gift of tongues, the gift of interpretation would be meaningless and useless. The Greek word here is *diermeneuō* (deeer-main-yoo-o) and it means to make the meaning clear, to explain the message, to expound upon the meaning, to translate into another language or vernacular for understanding.

Scriptural references for this gift are 1 Corinthians 12:30 and 14:5, 13, and 27. Interpretation is not only a gift of ministry for the unfolding of a mystery hidden in a foreign or unknown language, but is also a vital work (ministry) related to the expounding of the good news of Christ's coming. An example of the latter is found in Luke 24:27, which describes how Jesus interpreted the Old Testament Scriptures to the two disciples on the Emmaus road. Without question, the church has always needed this kind of clear interpretation. The gospel is too often stretched and twisted beyond recognition today. By their political schemes and theological systems and scientific principles, men take all sorts of undue liberties with the message of God's love in Christ for the world. Only sound interpretation will deliver the church from error.

Having said that, I do not confuse the normal, everyday meaning of "interpretation" with that peculiar gift of *diermeneuō*. This is the ability God gives some members of the body to hear, understand, and translate God's intended messages spoken in tongues so that the entire body can be built up and further equipped to serve as a redemptive agent for all people.

I would note these prominent characteristics of those who have the gift of interpretation. They appear to have received a meaning through a message spoken in an unknown tongue; their interpretation often coincides with rather familiar biblical passages. Often, however, they may feel they have heard no distinct message; thus, they tend to remain quiet or aloof, especially if they suspect that their gift or the speaker's gift may not be "operating." Contrasted to the speakers, these people tend to be more deliberative and meditative.

The Gift of Wisdom

This word, translated from the Greek *sophia* (so-fee-ah), means a practical application of knowledge (divine and natural) in specific and concrete situations that call for the grace (*charis*) or favor of God.

Related references are 1 Corinthians 12:8; Matthew 12:42; Acts 6:3, 10; 7:10; Colossians 1:28; 3:16; and 2 Peter 3:15. These show various applications of intelligence on a wide range of subjects. This gift is the ability God gives to some Christians to speak, utter, write, and/or paint words that bring insight, applying God's eternal and lofty truths to the daily living and ministering of the members.

Characteristically these gifted persons appear to have an uncanny ability to make statements which, at first, may not make sense, but get to the heart of a need. An example of this is Luther's oft-repeated phrase, "Love God and do as you please." Many times, these people do not realize the wisdom of their statements but feel compelled to speak their mind, often in spite of possible challenges or charges of being simple. They often have a way of saying something that brings to light the "hidden" but obvious truth. It simply "rings true."

Often the charismatically wise person, to the chagrin of others, asks practical questions or offers suggestions related to God's will, God's kingdom, and God's glory, which almost embarrass the rest of us with their sting of realism. An example of this is when our Lord wrote something in the sand as the adulteress was being subjected to public scrutiny (John 8:3–11). What he wrote we do not know, but it was enough to bring the accusers to the poignant reality of their own sins. They had a knowledge of the broader scope of God's laws and will, but could not see the particulars that related to them. Another example of one being able to tie broad and general knowledge of God's purposes to concrete realities was Paul's practical advice to sailors during a raging storm (Acts 27).

This gifted person has the ability not only to make a practical application of knowledge (*gnōsis*) given him by God or shared with him by another person, to concrete, specific situations. He is also able to glorify seemingly insignificant and natural situations by lifting them to the heights of divine reality. He can see, pronounce, and explain the presence of God in the most mundane and ordinary things and events. Simply put, his head is not so much in the clouds of theological mysteries that he cannot see God in the simple things in life. He comes across as a very practical person. For him, if God isn't in a marriage, a parent-child relationship, a business deal, "fun" things—and all the problems and joys related to these—then he isn't in heaven either! He does not see God as a "religious" being, but a participator in the rough and tumble of life, bringing repair, redemption, joy, love, and hope through and with the manifestation of the power and presence of the Holy Spirit.

9

Special Gifts

Singleness, Exorcism, Missionary, Witnessing, Music

WITH THE TWENTY-TWO GIFTS described in the foregoing chapters, we have considered all of those that are usually encountered in the literature of spiritual gifts. However, as I have stated, the list of gifts could go on almost interminably. In time, other gifts will perhaps be recognized as charismata and there are five which I particularly want to comment upon here.

The Gift of Singleness

My reason for including this among the gifts is twofold. Paul implies that the *charis* of God is a precondition for meaningful, productive singleness (1 Cor. 7:7), and the single person is free from the concerns of marriage so he or she may serve the Lord fully.

This gift, singleness, comes from the Greek word *agamos* (ag-a-mos) which means "to be unmarried, unattached, unbound." The scriptural base is found in 1 Cor. 7:32–35 and also can be seen by implication in verse 7.

In our society, no small amount of guilt has been imposed on those who have wished to remain single. Bad theology (thinking about God and man) has been the culprit here, in so far as the church is concerned. For so long we have been told that matrimony and parenthood are the unalterable will of God; otherwise, how could the human family be replenished? This has been the logic. Therefore, many have been coerced into marriage and parenthood who could have been healthier, happier, and more productive as singles. We all recognize this now. Paul, in Christ and with his gift of wisdom, gave us insight into the special grace of God for singleness nearly two thousand years ago.

Since the 1960s with all of the freedoms coming down the pike, quite a number of Christian men and women have discovered a joyful capability to remain single. And they have done so, not from a distaste for human fellowship or sexual intimacy or social involvement, but rather out of a need to concentrate interests and energies on a fuller intimacy with Christ and unhindered service to the church. This ability has also invaded the consciousness of the widowed and divorced.

I would define this gift as the motivation and ability God has given to some disciples to remain unbound by marriage in order to serve the body of Christ more fully and effectively.

The gift is unlike the rule of celibacy imposed on members of certain religious orders. To be sure, many of them are charismatic in their celibacy. Nevertheless, we must be reminded, *charis* is the free gift of God, given by him as a special and powerful favor in order to accomplish his purpose. It is not something that can be legislated or institutionalized; otherwise it is not free grace. So, we are not considering here an institutionalized celibacy. We are dealing only with the free grace of God that manifests itself in a person's desire to remain single for ministry purposes.

These gifted persons do not lose their sensitivity toward intimate relationships. They do not lose their consciousness of being sexual beings. But they discover a special power to keep intimacies and sexual drives under control. They feel pressured by the urgency of ministry situations that could be hampered and hurt by normal responsibilities in marriage and family life. They do not feel a morbid loneliness or intimacy deprivation, as do many coerced celibates, but a sense of joy and liberation over being free to serve the body of Christ.

It is interesting to note here that since the fifties and sixties and the great upsurge in openness to the baptism in the Holy Spirit, with the accompanying outpouring of charismata, many Roman Catholic priests and nuns have been liberated from an imposed celibacy (a Latin word for the state or condition of being unmarried or chaste, imposed by Gregory the Great at the end of the sixth century). Discovering ministry gifts that are not hindered by loving marriages and family living, they have left their orders to be married. On the other hand, many who have become single through death and divorce have discovered that *agamos* is their gift, and so they have remained single.

A word of encouragement is in order to those who have problems with this. I think of the young adult who told me that he wanted to remain single in order to serve God more fully, but was unable to control his sexual drives. Masturbation gave him the needed release, but left him racked by guilt.

If, indeed, this man has the gift of singleness—and is not single due to a lack of attractiveness or because of antisocial behavior (this needs to be checked out carefully)—God isn't playing a game with him. God has equipped each person to handle the gift he bestows, though perhaps not without suffering. We should expect to find in the exercise of the gift an adequate amount of joy, enough to sustain us in the midst of suffering. Guilt will destroy the joy (*chara*) of any gift. We should always remember that suffering does not have to be without joy. Suffering, itself, may be a part of the practice of one's gift. It may be that of all people, Christians who have discovered their gift that God has bestowed may be the most sensitive toward their sinful nature and their limitations. To have one gift, to be sure, means that we do not have other gifts; and the absence of other gifts makes us severely incomplete. But the joy is in the comforting presence of the Holy Spirit and in the strength, consolation, instruction, and correction contained in the charismata of others within the body of Christ. What my right arm cannot do, my left one can. If not, my legs or other parts of the body will come to the rescue. Suffering may be a vital dimension of a gift, but not without help (2 Cor. 12:1–10).

A lady, who may be representative of many others, described to me a severe bout with guilt over being meaningfully and joyfully widowed. She had loved her husband dearly and devotedly, and now, being a widow she had discovered her joy in being single and able to devote her remaining life to serving God.

"I ought to be missing my husband," she told me. "I loved him. I enjoyed being married to him. Why is it that I feel so liberated and enjoy what I can now do for God, and yet feel so guilty?"

It was a comfort to her to know that Paul went through the same conflicting struggle on many levels (see 2 Cor. 12:7–9), but came to the conclusion that the grace of God is sufficient.

Care must be taken here. We should not settle on something's being our gift for ministry until we have devoted enough time and experience to the confirmation process.

It is very important for us to realize that our knowledge of God is incomplete and mysterious; but it is not without confirming moments and events. Sensing our incompleteness, we often seek happiness at the exclusion of other valid emotions. One valid emotion may well be the guilt we feel over not missing a deceased loved one, or not being terribly lonely without him or her. But does anyone ever live up to married love's expectations?

The guilt feeling could be a way of saying: "I rarely felt that I was what I should have been as a wife; and my husband rarely lived up to what I expected of him. I don't want to cope with the past, so I'll ignore it entirely." To imagine that this pleasant feeling of ignoring the past, of not facing up to our limitations, is a charism is to invite some hard and painful moments ahead. The past needs to be worked through with much prayer and counseling.

However, on the other hand, it could very well be that a long-suppressed or disallowed charism of singleness has surfaced because of appropriate circumstances (widowhood). If this is the case, look for confirmations from God. As a gift is practiced and the gifted person matures, illicit feelings will fade away. The practice of one's gift, furthermore, should never be to gain deliverance from or to acquire feelings or emotions of any kind, but to be loyal to Christ in a shared ministry. Then and only then can the process lead to the upbuilding of the body of Christ and not to self-aggrandizement or mere selfish pleasure.

The Gift of Exorcism

I know that many of my colleagues will question my including this among the gifts. But my reasoning is based on the New Testament evidence of evil spirits and demon possession; also, the presence of evil spirits today is indisputable, thus requiring effective activity against them.

There are some subjects in the New Testament about which we are strangely quiet today. And it isn't difficult for us to figure out why this is so. One reason is our hang-up on a scientific world view that does not allow speculations beyond what can be materially analyzed and evaluated. So much of our own present-day practice of the Christian faith is restricted to whatever is scientifically acceptable. This comes from the basic Aristotelian view which says that reality rests in the senses, that nothing deserves our attention unless it relates to that which can be seen, tasted, touched, smelled, and heard.

A chemist, George Price, writing in *Science* about extrasensory perception said, "No intelligent man can read the evidence for the existence of ESP and doubt that it exists, but, since we know it is impossible, we must conclude that all this evidence is due to error and fraud." We have become so prejudiced against certain things that, though there is evidence of their presence and power, we easily dismiss even the obvious as error and fraud because it is not fashionable to think otherwise. Many people I know would not be "caught dead" reading a book on charismata, to say nothing of evil spirits and demons. Yet these same people say that science has failed to offer any help in these matters, which they cannot easily dismiss.

There is another view of reality, and it comes from the New Testament. Jesus apparently believed in a dynamic reality that comes from a nonphysical source—the spiritual, if you will. According to the Gospels, Jesus believed in and conversed with angels and demons—the references number more than 190 in the Gospels. Who among us would say that Jesus was wrong or psychotic? Paul followed our Lord's teachings concerning man's reach for God and God's coming to man, and he explained man's significant role in the struggle between the forces of right and the forces of evil that reside beyond but invade human flesh (Eph. 6:14; Acts 16:16–18).

The Greek word for "exorcist" is *exorkistes* (ex-er-kistays). Various forms of this word are used throughout the New Testament. It means basically, to send out, to leave, to expel, to cast out, to let go, to release, to call forth, to diffuse, to extricate, to free.

It is obvious from the many Bible references that demons or evil spirits require a form of treatment different from that offered through the spiritual gift of healings. To be possessed by an evil spirit was and is not a normal illness, nor is it purely a psychological hang-up. It is a state of being bound by an alien force.

In all of recorded history, man has recognized this to a great extent and consequently has developed magical formulas, incantations, brews, and rituals in his attempts to expel evil spirits. The Jews of our Lord's day had their problems with their attempts at exorcism. Their rituals and superstitious activities became tools of the devil, putting them into a double bind.

The method our Lord used to expel demons was the power of a word of authority (Matt. 8:16). His disciples patterned their work after Jesus' example, and did it "in the name of Jesus" (Mark 16:17, Luke 10:17). How they delivered people from demon possession is a far cry from the ways many claim to use today, with their long cries of "Jeeeeeeeeessuss," their loud commands, slapping the possessed, their use of pencil tracings and handkerchiefs and "points of contact" (asking the afflicted to touch their television sets while prayer is being offered a thousand miles away). One wonders how Jesus and the disciples ever succeeded without tents, mailings, microphones, healing temples, and TV cameras!

We should be concerned about the timidity of reasonable and informed Christians who decline comment about the possibility of actual demon possession today. In the few discussions I have had with my fellow ministers about such a possibility, none of them has made an out-and-out denial that there is such a thing. But the aura was one of timidity and confusion. I know where they are coming from or, let us say, where they are in their not going anywhere—I was there for a long time. My training was in liberal theology and clinical psychology (the psychology being based on the Rogerian technique of nondirective counseling, the pastoral theology being based on the mode of the 1950s—facilitating and enabling ministries). I believed that the ills of the world could be solved with the preaching of love, justice, and brotherhood, and supplementing those with deeds of mercy, social services, and the right liturgy. It took me a long time— twenty-four years—to confess how burned out I was, how bankrupt I had become. How I longed for the authoritative word of Jesus or someone "in the name of Jesus" to release me from a bondage I was in, but could not describe! It happened, but in solo fashion.

After an eight-week struggle all the way to hell and back, finally being willing to look at myself as God presented me to me, piece by piece, I was lying in the middle of the floor in a pitch-dark bedroom telling God that I was through fighting him and hurting myself, I had fought the "unbeatable foe," had given up dreaming the "impossible dream"—the "scorn" and "scars" were more than I could bear, and I wanted to die. I was through with him, with life, with me. At that moment, in the thick blackness of the midnight hour, I saw and felt an even blacker thing move up through and out of me, leaving in its wake a peace and calm I never dreamed existed. I watched the "thing" as it silently moved upward from my body and vanished in the darkness.

It would be verbally impossible to describe what began to change in my life. Suffice it to say, nearly every aspect of my life and faith took a 180-degree turn. I had been possessed by something that was alien to God's will for my life. I was now emptied of it. A new beginning was given me. That was three years ago and I praise God now, hundreds of times every day and night. My life is turned around now. Virtually everything is approached from a different attitude—prayer, Scripture, devotions, hard work and long hours, loving and appreciating (without using) others, serving the church for what I may be privileged to offer rather than for political and status aspirations—and I am actually dreading the day when retirement is forced upon me. I am not where I want to be, but it is great fun to be in process.

And I wonder how many others are similarly bound! C. S. Lewis has helped us overcome the image of the devil with horns and tail by describing him as the Bible does, as an angel of light. But it is going to take more than fiction and masterful writings to deliver us from the satanic forces that bind us. Our Lord is in that business today. And I believe he has a gift for the church that can deliver its people from the mounting subtle evils . . . in his name.

The Gift of Missionary

Without question, there is much evidence of a special ability that God has given to certain members of the body of Christ to move across the boundaries of race, color, creed, language, geography, culture subcultures, and life-styles to serve basic needs of others as a means of demonstrating the love of Christ. This is not the same as *apostolos* (apostle), one sent out as a messenger or herald of good news about Christ, nor the *euaggelistes* (evangelist), one who preaches with a passion and effectiveness to win others to Christ. This is a person who is equipped with special talents and acquired skills who can serve the neglected basic needs of segments of God's family.

I hope this description helps the reader understand why this special gift is being separated from the others which may be similar. The apostle and the evangelist are special ministry gifts that relate people to the redemptive character and caring fellowship of his church. The missionary gift, however, is the enfleshment of the gospel in unselfish acts of directly serving the more basic needs of others across the already stated boundaries: feeding the hungry, clothing the naked, healing the sick, sheltering the homeless, protecting the weak, working for peace, building roads, improving land and livestock, training the unskilled, translating Bibles and other vital literature, and many, many other services.

In a great respect, this gift resembles some of the others, such as service, helps, giving, hospitality, leadership, administration, and healing. But the main difference is that this gift of missionary (a term used for the lack of a better one) is one that motivates someone who may have one or more of those gifts to go into other cultures for fulfillment.

The behavioral characteristics are such that they hear the call to other peoples and are moved by the needs that are not generally known. They experience no trepidation (or so it appears) about going into the unknown and unfamiliar and they delight in new challenges. They dream of making things better for the less fortunate in other places; they find it relatively easy to learn new customs and languages; they have no fear of living only with basic tools and supplies, and few personal amenities. They have an uncanny notion that they can make a difference in the lives of those they serve; they do not necessarily feel the need to verbalize their faith, believing that the manner of doing conveys a quality of compassion that words may not always communicate. Love to them is something that is done, not always something said.

I do not want this to sound as though I preclude the combination of speaking and doing. Rather, it is my intent to point out the large body of evidence that indicates that many people are extremely effective and find great fulfillment in serving others in life's basic and often neglected needs. Jesus' own teaching commends such: " ' "Lord, when did we see thee hungry and feed thee, or thirsty and give thee drink? And when did we see thee a stranger and welcome thee, or naked and clothe thee?" . . . And the King will answer them, "Truly, I say to you, as you did it to one of the least of these my brethren, you did it to me" ' " (Matt. 25:37–40).

The Gift of Witness

Every disciple of Christ has the responsibility and privilege of sharing his or her witness to Christ (Acts 1:8). This is not something that can be taken lightly. It is so important and requires such a degree of intentionality that Jesus offered the power of the Holy Spirit to make it possible and effective. Paul, in like manner, said that ". . . no one can say 'Jesus is Lord' except by the Holy Spirit" (1 Cor. 12:3). It is the role of every Christian to share his or her faith in Christ with others.

But there are others who are called by God to be a special kind of witness. These are they who may be privileged to witness through hardships and even death. Church history is rich with examples of this. Stephen was the first (see Acts 6:8–7:60) to die for his witness, followed by an innumerable host (see *Foxe's Book of Martyrs*).

The Greek verb for this is *marturomai* (mar-too-rah-mahee), meaning to give a witness, to give an account, to declare solemnly, to give one's life as a witness to Christ. This last part is what comes to mind when we hear or see the word *martyr*, the root word for "witness." Scriptural references to this kind of witnessing are plentiful, with the following as a few examples: Acts 5:27–42; 12:1–11; 22:1–25; 1 Corinthians 13:3; 2 Corinthians 11:21–30; 12:7–10; and Revelation 2:13.

We are touched and moved by these witnesses and the multitude of others who were tortured and killed for their faith in Christ. But we know of many, many more who are not blessed by a quick death. They suffer long for their faith. They must go on living day-by-day and for a lifetime under painful and trying pressures that come from opposition to their faith in Christ. Yet, they live with a joy and special strength, as well as influence for Christ. Their gift is the power to endure hardships caused by their faith in such a way that other members of the body of Christ are strengthened with encouragement and others are won to Christ by their witness.

Some characteristics of these witnesses are: they are single-minded in their purpose to serve Christ no matter what; they are "stubborn" in that they believe in and will not depart from their purpose to serve Christ; they accept hardships and suffering as being under the care and design of God; their expressions of joy drown out temptations to complain; hope is a key to their endurance; when they think of dying, it is in terms of "for" something, not "with" something; and, for the most part, their thoughts and intentions are focused on what they are living "for" and not "with."

The Gift of Music

Certain people, after experiencing an intense spiritual awakening or baptism of the Holy Spirit, suddenly seem to have acquired musical ability. Previously they showed little or no particular aptitude for music, but now they write lyrics and/or musical scores, or sing, or take up an instrument. I have known some of these gifted people myself. Before they received the Spirit into their lives, they could not read or play music. But upon being led of God to write or to play music, they discovered a rare ability.

They produce rhymes, rhythms, and musical pieces that bring considerable blessing to many. I have seen such people play the piano or guitar, or sing, and I have been unable to explain their giftedness apart from their new relationship with God.

While I was senior pastor of the University United Methodist Church, in Chapel Hill, North Carolina, a beautiful but relatively uneducated black woman came to see me. She asked for a sheet of paper and pen and after a brief prayer, she began to write in a "language" she did not understand. After another brief prayer, she wrote the translation of it, a simple but beautiful psalm-type praise of God. She demonstrated this ability several times. The reason she came to me was because she had already been to the professors in the languages department of the university and they had seen nothing they recognized. She thought a "man of God" might help. But she went away disappointed.

On another day she came back and asked if I would accompany her into the sanctuary. My associates and I went in and gave her an audience. God, she claimed, had given her another gift—that of singing in an unknown tongue. After a brief prayer at the kneeling rail, she sang something unbelievably beautiful. After she was finished, an associate asked if she could sing it in English, which she did after another brief prayer. It was a most beautiful praise to God.

In another church two years later, two ladies visited my office with similar gifts. One had the gift of writing and playing piano music, something she had never done until she was "baptized with the Holy Spirit." The other lady had begun to compose lyrics and musical scores that she sang while playing the guitar. Both claimed to have "boxes of the stuff." They said that they often awakened from sleep and "heard" these songs which they would write down or record with a tape recorder.

Such people seem to have certain characteristics in common: they believe in and experience the presence of the Holy Spirit; they "hear" the music as Mozart claimed he did; they must obey the inclination or inspiration immediately or they lose the "piece"; they do not use or display what they receive until it has been confirmed in the Scriptures; what they compose resembles or uses actual scriptural language; and they believe the music is given as a message to someone or a group.

Summary

I do not move about in Pentecostal circles, but the God of Pentecost has certainly moved into and encircled my life. What happened to me three years ago was nothing that I sought or wanted.

I had become convinced that there was nothing more that I could experience, and that mine had been a wasted career spreading over three decades and several churches, in two states and on two continents. I had preached before large congregations and assemblies, and in prominent pulpits—including John Wesley's in Wesley's Chapel, London. I had conducted weddings and funerals for prominent heart surgeons and high governing officials. I had stood before university students, professors, deans, and presidents as a preacher and served them as priest. I had traveled throughout Europe and debated Communists in the Soviet Union, Czechoslovakia, and Poland. I thought there was nothing more to do or to experience and had come to the place where it all seemed so senseless and futile. I was on the way out of the ministry for I did not know what I believed and could not make any sense out of prayer. The Bible was strange and beyond my comprehension. To me, the church was nothing more than any other sociological institution; in intelligence and productivity, it was perhaps less. It had become to me a politically poor, economically greedy, and educationally inept encumbrance in the community.

But into that morass of mentality and chaos of conscience God came with his awakening, forgiving, repairing grace. And with this new life came reminders of those special messengers of God who faithfully touched my life with their gifts along the way. Some had come to me with complaints and some with compliments; some with rebukes and some with retorts; some with silence and some with songs; some with thanks and some with thoughts; some with gentility and some with grunts; some with groanings and others with guts; some with fumblings and some with finesse; some with rank and some with reasoning; some with dares and some with dreams; some with tears and some with trembling; some with Bibles and others with bowed heads; some with prayers and others with pleas. But God had sent them all as gifts to enrich my life.

Gifts are powerful. They work when they are worked. We may never see the results or reap the harvest. But what joy there is in believing and hoping someday someone's life may be touched and tamed by a gift of ministry faithfully used!

God's gifts are innumerable. Their variety is as wide as our acceptance. Let us not limit them with a small faith.

"As each has received a gift, employ it for one another, as good stewards of God's varied grace; whoever speaks . . . whoever renders service . . . that in everything God may be glorified through Jesus Christ. To him belong glory and dominion for ever and ever. Amen" (1 Pet. 4:10, 11).

10

Gifts, Acts of Sacramental Obedience

THE WORD *sacrament* is a medieval word. Though it is used in official doctrine and practice by most denominations, it is not a New Testament word. But so it is with many theological terms, such as *Trinity.* How many churches go by that name, though it is not found in the New Testament.

Sacrament is a rich word that communicates a meaning to us no other word can. In the discussion that follows I am using the word to convey an outward and visible sign of an inward, spiritual grace of the Lord Jesus Christ.

Generally speaking, a sacrament is a means by which the grace of God is transmitted to an obedient follower of Jesus Christ. Unfortunately, from the inception of the concept by Augustine, bishop of Hippo (395-430 A.D.), the church has not been able to make up its mind as to how many sacraments there are. The twelfth-century church fathers identified as many as thirty, and the Council of Trent (1545-64) dropped the number to seven. The Reformation churches brought a further reduction of the number to two,

namely baptism and the Lord's Supper, or Holy Communion. Some sects refused to acknowledge any sacraments,
or their value, saying that they are manmade ways of con-
trolling and manipulating constituents.

But *sacrament* is better understood when it is seen in
light of its root or origin in the word *mystery, mysterion.*
When the New Testament was translated into Latin, the
Greek word *mysterion* became *sacramentum.* To be sure,
we all know that a "mystery" is something that has a rugged
reality in experience but defies explanation. The writer of
Ephesians uses *mysterion* often as he speaks of Christ (*see*
3:4; 5:32; 6:19). He knew that something extraordinary was
happening to those who are intimately related to Christ,
but he could only describe it as a *mysterion.*

When we come to this matter of receiving spiritual gifts
and obediently using them we run into another cloud of
mystery. As one uses a gift in faithful obedience, something
begins to operate vividly and manifestly, not only in his
or her life but also in, for, and among the body of believers
(Eph. 4:10–16).

My logic says that if a sacrament is a "sign" or "means"
or "expression" of the inward, spiritual grace of our Lord
Jesus Christ, and if the spiritual gift (*charisma* or *pneumati-
kōs* or *doma*) is a grace-gift from Christ for the edification
of the church, then the blend of a person and his or her
faithful practice of the gift becomes a sacrament. I see no
difference between this gift of grace and the grace that Holy
Communion and baptism offer.

What this means to me is that people who use their special
grace-gift properly (Eph. 4:16; 1 Pet. 4:10) become sacraments as we define the term. This also suggests to me that
there are as many different sacraments as there are people
who obediently use their spiritual gifts. Furthermore, this
sheds new light on the sacramental nature of Christian fellowship (*koinonia*) and community life. The fellowship

of the mutually sharing community becomes, in essence, a sacrament in all of its manifestations and ministries. I am not talking about the institutionalization of the grace of Christ that happened in the medieval church. I am talking about the assembly of individuals who alone possess "differing gifts" (Rom. 12:4–8), the whole of which is greater than the sum of the parts.

A word of caution is necessary here. An error in thinking and practice has occurred among many who claim to have gifts. Rugged individualism and uninformed charismatism have caused fellowship to sour, churches to split, and good news to become bad. It is difficult to determine which is the greater evil: uninformed and individualistic charismatism or deliberate denial of the special grace of God for today's ministries.

Through obedience to the gospel of Christ we become the outward and visible sign of an inward and spiritual grace of Jesus Christ. Obedience, then, is the key—not blind or naive, but deliberate and informed. Through such obedience to Christ we become carriers of his grace to bless hundreds and thousands of others as we become what he has designed us to be (1 Cor. 15:10). Only by this obedience can we be more than what we are (in the flesh) and do more than what we can (Phil. 4:13). Sacramental (charismatic) obedience is the only means by which our eyes become our Lord's eyes, our heart becomes his heart, and our hands and feet become his hands and feet (Rom. 12:1). Sacramental or charismatic obedience is the only means by which the church (*ekklesia*) or assembly of devotees of Christ becomes the very body of Christ in and for the world today (Col. 1:18).

I realize that this is a great mystery, but it is no more a mystery (perhaps less) than what Paul talks about in 1 Corinthians 10:16, 17, when he speaks of the mysterious connection between Christ and his followers gathered to celebrate his broken body and shed blood. How the dead physical body of Jesus can become incarnate in the simple act of eating bread and drinking wine is, indeed, mysterious. But we believe and experience that something happens when we obey his command, " 'Do this in remembrance of me' " (1 Cor. 11:24). Paul said, "This is a great mystery, and I take it to mean Christ and the church . . ." (Eph. 5:32).

I have been talking about the charismata or spiritual gifts as being special manifestations of the grace of God. A great mystery—a *sacramentum,* if you will. What I want to move to now is a discussion of the necessary preparation for the sacrament. And I want to do this with the aid of a very simple, perhaps childish, acronym based on what I have already referred to as the essence of a sacrament: *obedience.* Whatever happens in a sacrament doesn't happen without belief (preparation) and practice (doing it). As a device to aid in our preparation for and practice of the spiritual gift, we use the letters OBEDIENCE, and the word each letter represents, to begin our preparation and practice.

"O"—OBEY GOD'S CALLING

In Romans 11:29 Paul says that the "gifts and the call of God are irrevocable." In 1 Corinthians 12:7 and 1 Peter 4:10 we are assured that each has been given a spiritual or grace-gift. The word *calling* in Romans 11:29, *klesis,* means to be invited or designated by name. This personalizes the gift that is distributed to a person (1 Cor. 12:11). The word *irrevocable* means, of course, unchangeable or without turning back. As free moral agents, possessing a volitional will, we are not forced by God to accept any of his gifts or callings. If we refuse, we do so at the cost or loss of our wholeness (salvation). And we cannot be whole (saved) without accepting all he has to offer. So the first step in preparation, discovery, and practice of our gift and calling is OBEDIENCE.

"B"—BEGIN A STUDY OF THE GIFTS

It is a generally accepted adage that "a call to ministry is a call to prepare." This principle has been applied to those who are called to the ordained ministry. I contend that every person has the calling to a ministry (Rom. 11:20; Eph. 4:7–16). Therefore, it is essential for everyone to take his calling and gift seriously enough to make proper preparation for an effective ministry (Eph. 4:16).

Paul exhorts his young friend and protégé, Timothy, not to neglect his gift, to stir up the gift by bold and powerful use of it, and to study his responsibility so as to be properly equipped (1 Tim. 4:14; 2 Tim. 1:6, 7; 2:15). From this we gather that though the gift is given, it is still our responsibility to maintain an awareness of its value and power in the body of Christ for edification. We infer from Paul's counsel that the gift can become ineffective and shame-producing from a lapse in use or understanding.

But prior even to this, a study of the varieties, possible uses, and results of gifts (1 Cor. 12:4–6) can help one discover his particular gift or gifts. Unfortunately, we are not as unencumbered by generations of misunderstandings and denials of spiritual gifts as were first-generation Christians. We, therefore, stand in need of some reconditioning. We need to become open to the prospects of the New Testament's testimony to the varieties of gifts. While New Testament Christians needed only to open themselves in obedience to the presence and power of the Holy Spirit (1 Cor. 12:7) for the reality of a gift to manifest itself, we find it necessary to study and to rethink our position back through a lot of bad theology regarding fresh and daily experiences of God.

It is sad to learn that after some two thousand years most members of many churches know very little about the Holy Spirit and less about the manifestations (*phanerōsis*) of the Holy Spirit in the form of spiritual gifts (1 Cor. 12:7). In the many workshops I have conducted on discovering gifts no more than one in twenty persons (including pastors—seminary trained!) had ever heard about the gifts. Fewer knew what their gift was. Our work is cut out for us! A study is absolutely essential before all of us discover the gifts present in the body of Christ. Beginning a study is to assure ourselves of the discovery.

There are three ways to make such a study. The first is to run the references in the New Testament. If one knows Greek, he will find it exciting to look up the words *charis, charisma, charismata, charizomai, charitoō, pneuma, pneumatikos, dōrea, dōreomai, dōron, doma,* and *domata.* If one does not know Greek, any good Greek-English or English-Greek dictionary or concordance can assist here.

Another way of studying the gifts is to read the books that are listed in the bibliography at the end of this book. Until 1972, only one author, Donald Gee, had published a book on this subject. Since then, however, some seventy or eighty books have been published—some good and some not so good—and most of them do increase our understanding. Many "heavyweight" theologians are producing fine works on the subject.

A third suggestion for study is to observe the lives of persons you know who possess and obediently use the gift(s) God has given. This is not difficult to do after a thorough study of the New Testament references and the behavioral characteristics of the various gifts. The life of a person is the best raw material and primary source of any study.

"E"—EXAMINE FEELINGS AND FANTASIES

One sure way of getting "into" the sacrament of Holy Communion as a reenactment (remembrance) of the death of our Lord and letting it become a true sacrament is to visualize the actual crucifixion of Christ as one receives the bread and wine, and then to examine one's feelings.

So often, this sacrament becomes cold and mechanical because we fail to use our imaginations and feelings. One way of overcoming this is to begin an inward conversation on the way to the altar, or as the elements are being distributed, saying to oneself, "How do I feel about partaking in the death of my Lord? How does it feel to be going to his crucifixion? What's going to happen to me as I drink his blood and eat his flesh? Is it going to matter to me? Will it make a difference in my relationship to him? In my life? In my living for him? Do I know what this means to me and the others who are partaking? Do I know what Paul meant when he said, 'I have been crucified with Christ; it is no longer I who live, but Christ who lives in me; and the life I now live in the flesh I live by faith in the Son of God, who loved me and gave himself for me' (Galatians 2:20)?" The principle here is not to stop one's thinking and imaging with the words of the leader of worship, but to feel one's way into the reenactment of the event being celebrated.

Someone has said that God must have loved water—he created an awful lot of it! The same could be said about feelings. God gave us an abundance of them. In fact, modern psychology says that most—some 90 percent—of one's life is lived on the basis of how he feels about things. Fantasies, a component of feeling, are initiators and stimulators for the structuring or conceptualizing of feelings into qualitative and quantitative forms. Feelings and fantasies are important to the discovery and use of spiritual gifts.

As we study the varieties, uses, and results of gifts, it is important for us to evaluate each gift on the basis of how we feel about it. One way to set the feelings soaring is to fantasize the possession, use, and desired results of the one under study. The psalmist in Psalm 37:4 said that it is okay to exercise a feeling: "Take delight in the Lord, and he will give you the desires of your heart." This is to say that it would be of value to attempt to apply the feeling of joy to our possible possession and use of a gift.

This is, however, not to suggest that we stand in a cafeteria line before a counter full of charismata available for the choosing. It is, rather, to suggest, as Luther once put it, "Love God and do as you please," which really means that to love God is to want to do only that which pleases God. Feelings can be an avenue in which God is guiding us to do what pleases him.

It is a terrible teaching that says we are not to enjoy loving God or delight in doing his will. God, perhaps more often than not, plants his will deep in our hearts, and as it is allowed to blossom, its beauty expresses itself in a perpetuating desire. As we study to discover the gift God has given us, let us ask, "What do I feel? What really excites me most as I fantasize serving God fully and faithfully?"

I must share a further word about one of the most trustworthy feelings God has given to us—joy. The New Testament writers use this expressive word and the verb form, "rejoice," no less than one hundred times. As I was researching the word *charism* and began to break it down in its component stems, I was startled to discover something that explains much of the ecstasy that often accompanies knowing and using spiritual gifts. The basic word, *charis,* which means grace or favor of God, becomes grace-gift or gifts of grace when the suffix *ma* or *mata* is added. And built into the word is the stem, *char,* meaning "joy." A basic element in charismata then is joy, one of the fruits of the Spirit (Gal. 5:22).

Just because a person may have discovered his or her gift and is obediently using it doesn't mean that the practice of the gift is without difficulty. In fact, faithfully using a gift may be a most difficult, if not painful, undertaking. But God has designed the gift to be undergirded by the sustaining and motivating power of joy. Thus, ". . . the joy of the Lord is your strength" (Neh. 8:10).

"D"—DARE TO COMMIT YOURSELF TO THE GIFT

To believe something is to commit oneself to that something. Belief is a state of mental and emotional activity that requires an object. It is not something that one possesses, but what he wills. Thinking, feeling, and willing constitute the essence of living. I have attempted to show that feeling something is important. Likewise it is important to realize that the power behind *feeling* is the act of *willing.* In discovering and preparing to make use of a gift, it is essential to activate the will toward what 1 Corinthians 12:7, Romans 12:6, Ephesians 4:7, and 1 Peter 4:10 say about each person having a gift. The matter of willing to commit oneself to a particular gift—even before knowing that the gift is his—is necessary in testing the thinking and feeling.

I have heard people say, "Well, God must not have given me a gift," or "I'm not that important to receive a gift." This is either a deliberate denial of God's Word, the Bible, or self-willed ignorance, for the Lord says, "As each has received a gift, employ it for one another, as good stewards of God's varied grace. . ." (1 Pet. 4:10). Many people appear to try to be humble about their possessing a special gift by denying that they have one; but in reality they slander the Word of God that says without equivocation "each one" has a gift. A correction of these errors is to:

Obey the call by opening yourself to God's Word
Begin a study of the possibilities
Examine your feelings in light of what you've studied
Dare to commit yourself to the one that delights you.

"I"—INVESTIGATE THE GIFTS OF OTHERS

It is one thing to study the Bible and other literature
on this subject. But it is another to study the lives of those
who are known to possess certain gifts. Paul used this technique when he instructed young Timothy to remember the
faith of his grandmother Lois and his mother Eunice,
"which," said Paul, "now, I am sure, dwells in you" (2
Tim. 1:5). Paul was not talking about the general faith that
all Christians possess, but the special gift (charism) of faith
that performs miracles (1 Cor. 12:9). Paul repeatedly reminded his readers of his own gifts, perhaps not calling
them such, but certainly illustrating their presence and importance in his own life.

This discussion is placed here, following a consideration
of the behavioral characteristics associated with each of the
gifts, so that we may be able to recognize the gifts in others.
Many people possess and use their gifts in ways that are
easily recognizable, though they themselves may not have
a name for their gifts. Being a "gift hunter" has become
an exciting pastime to me. Taking what information I have
accumulated about certain of the gifts, I look for them in
the people I meet. I study their actions, their manner of
speaking, and the results of their service to Christ and his
church, and to my amazement I discover some who think
they are absolutely talentless, but who are unbelievably
effective in their service to Christ. What they are actually
accomplishing for Christ can't be explained except by the
presence and use of grace-gifts. After studying such people,
I am convinced that God does distribute his extraordinary
powers to people today.

The principle here is to look for the gifts in others and

let them be a possible example for your own experimentation (Heb. 13:7).

"E"—EXPERIMENT WITH THE GIFTS YOU THINK YOU MAY HAVE

There is nothing wrong with desiring something related to Christ. Without a desire, you may never find the very thing you need. The process goes from desire, to action, to results. Sometimes the result may be learning that a certain gift is not the right one, that God did not intend for it to be yours. This is why experimentation is important.

Paul sets us the example. He had an intense desire to be freed of a "thorn in the flesh" (2 Cor. 12:1–10), but he discovered through praying that the "thorn" was a means of receiving a grace of God sufficient to transcend any weakness. He would have never known that special grace and power had he not experimented by prayers for deliverance.

The method for discovering a spiritual gift is similar to that of discovering a natural ability or talent—you've got to try it to find out whether or not it is for you.

A world-famous healer and teacher, early in his experience with the Holy Spirit, believed that everyone could and should speak in tongues. He was always urging his four preacher-brothers to seek this gift. One of them, a dear friend of mine, told a class of pastors that for a long time he thought something was wrong with him or his salvation because he never felt the urge to speak in tongues. One day, he said, while driving alone in his car, he opened his mouth, stuck out his tongue, and said, "Here I am, Lord. Here's my tongue. I am willing. Do it! Touch my tongue and give me *the* blessing."

But nothing happened. He tried this several times, but to no avail. He finally concluded that tongues was not his gift when he understood Paul's words that one gift is given to this person, another to that person, and that no one gift is meant for all of us (see 1 Cor. 12:8–11). He found out by experimenting what gift he did not have.

Another dear friend of mine felt peculiarly moved in the presence of Christian friends who were ill. One day this became very intense until she felt compelled to ask a friend who had been deaf in one ear for twenty or more years to let her pray for her hearing. Her friend consented to the laying on of hands and a special prayer, and was immediately healed. Neither the lady healed nor the healer would have known the presence and blessing of the gift if my friend had not been willing to experiment.

The principle here is that it is just as important to discover what gifts you do not have as it is to learn what gift you do have, and that one sure way of finding out is to experiment.

"N"—NEVER DOUBT GOD'S WORD AND PROMISES

Many times I ask, "Do you really want to discover a special power that can transcend your experienced weaknesses?" And the answer quickly comes: "Yes!"

I ask further, "Would you like to know that you have a beauty and power that education, position, and material abundance have not been able to satisfy?" And again the answer comes very quickly, in the affirmative. I do not find many people who are satisfied with what they are inwardly and outwardly—even those who are faithful members of the church. But at the same time, I don't find many who understand the value of taking God's Word, as we know it in the Bible, seriously. I have discovered anew the value of the Bible in my own life. This did not come about as a result of someone else's influence on me, but as a matter of course, when I unreservedly threw myself open to the Bible as being God's Word, not simply "containing" the Word of God. I rediscovered a Word that did not rely on anything other than itself to interpret itself—a Word that really cannot be taught unless it is "caught," by living out and acting out its claims—a Word that was not only inspired in the writing, but is also inspiring in the reading—a Word whose authority and power mix actively with the faith and obedience of the believer.

I am not talking about a literalism or a biblicism that stumbles over dates, names, events, words, and sequence. I am talking about a commitment to the Bible's revelation of a God and Savior who seeks faith and commitment and in return gives changed hearts, minds, and lives. I don't worry now over the different views people hold toward the Bible—the fundamentalist versus the modernist, or the inerrantist–errantist, or the divinely inspired–inspirationalist approaches. I simply throw myself before the Word and open myself without reservation or restriction to whatever happens. I no longer believe what the Bible says is true simply because it is in the Bible. Rather, I believe in the truth of the Bible because of what happens to me when I unreservedly commit myself to what it says.

The principle I am suggesting here is to challenge any doubt about what the New Testament says concerning the gifting of God by simple, but strong, commitment. Refusing to allow doubt to dominate will lead to the joy of commitment. Believe, therefore, that God has gifted you; act and behave according to that belief; and you are well on your way toward discovery.

"C"—CENSURE ALL NOTIONS OF PRIDE OVER GIFTS

Standing against God's promises and their fulfillment is the devastating danger of pride. Too many churches have been bifurcated and reduced to an inadequate fellowship through constant conflicts due to feelings of superiority and inferiority. Paul tells us that thinking too highly of ourselves and too lowly of others has no place in the body of Christ (Rom. 12:3; 1 Cor. 13:4; Phil. 2:3, 4).

To be gifted by God is a high privilege. To be delivered

from sin, liberated from debilitating selfishness, and empowered with the presence of God's purposive grace for specialized service is to know how privileged we are. But this is
no warrant for pride—only sacramental obedience.

The gifts are not given as special favors to those who
show great promise, or as a reward for faithfulness. They
are given for ministry to other members of the body of
Christ and to others, including God, through the body.

If there is a ranking notion to be found, it is in the discovery that ministry never means "more" or "greater," but
"less" or "lesser" (minus-try). Originally, the term *ministry*
described the work of a slave for his master, a soldier for
his king, an employee for his employer. If we follow this
in the major passages covering gifts for ministry we can
see how impossible it would be for any form of ministry
to position itself over another. All ministry gifts work under
the headship of Jesus Christ, in equality, with unity and
harmony, for mutual upbuilding.

To obey God is to accept what is given. When this acceptance truly manifests an ability or power not known before,
it is easy to become enamored of the gift or results and to
forget the Giver. This was the subject of the "Corinthian
error" (1 Cor. 12:3) wherein two sides of a congregation
engaged in vituperation and condemnation. Both of them
lost sight of the fact that gifts, services, and results are
mere manifestations of a greater gift, the Spirit. To deny
the value, stature, and results of any other's particular gift
is to denigrate the very Spirit, the source of real living.

All gifts are given for the common good of all members
of the body of Christ, and never for self-aggrandizement,
independence, or self-fulfillment. The wholeness of the
body and its corporate ministries to its community and to
the world should always be uppermost in all that we do.
The censuring of any thoughts of self-gain or display is a
vital part of the gifts-discovery process.

"E"—EXPECT GOD TO PRODUCE RESULTS

This is that for which we have yearned, for which we have become obedient. This is that for which God has given us gifts.

God produces the results of our gifts. We can only offer ourselves as living vessels and channels (Rom. 12:1). God is the God of the harvest, the results. Paul says, "Therefore, my beloved, as you have always *obeyed,* so now . . . work out your own salvation with fear and trembling; for God is at work in you, both to will and to work for his good pleasure" (Phil. 2:12, 13). It is God's good pleasure that we seek.

I do not believe anyone who has come this far in his journey in discipleship, to the point of realizing that a special power or gift for building up the body of Christ is offered him, wants anything other than what God wills for his life. To be sure, many have sought in their relationship with God what they wanted and believed they were entitled to, but eventually it could only be gained at the cost of their gift and faith. To seek after anything other than God's will and pleasure is to travel a road that leads to defeat. This is why it is important to remember that a spiritual gift is never for the pleasure or profit of the recipient, but for one purpose: to glorify God (1 Pet. 4:11). This always produces God's intended results. Our participation through obedience frees God to bring about what he has designed.

We do not always know what happens as the result of our obedience and we do not have to know, in order to be obedient. The faith that every person has, that motivates him to discover and to put to use his special spiritual gift, will also equip him to trust God for whatever occurs beyond the joy and splendor of obedience. The principle then is whatever you do, do it to God's glory: "To him belong glory and dominion for ever and ever. Amen" (1 Pet. 4:11).

11

Practical Means for Discovering Your Gift

IN THIS CHAPTER I want to explore strategies or techniques that are often used in discovering the gifts and outline a workshop pastors and other leaders may use to facilitate discovery.

In the preceding chapter on OBEDIENCE, I attempted not only to show that the practice or faithful use of a gift is a sacrament, an outward and visible sign of an inward, spiritual grace; but also I tried to aid in the discovery of a gift by urging obedience to the calling (Rom. 11:29). I believe this is all one needs to discover his gift. But other methods and techniques may prove helpful.

1. *A Workshop on Spiritual Gifts.* I will be saying more about this in the suggested outline, but for now I want to emphasize the importance of the intentional effort put forth in a special seminar or workshop setting. This usually requires some six hours followed by a church school class or other study group meeting for a longer period.

The objective of the workshop—helping members of the body discover their gift(s) and thus lead the entire congregation into the discovery and exercise of gifts—is so vital that the workshop leader must give careful attention to the recruitment of participants. Some people will attend anything the church sponsors, simply out of their need for fellowship. While fellowship should be offered by any church, it is obviously not the purpose of a seminar like this. If you want to conduct such a workshop, you will want to devote several months to the planning. You will not want to rely on the church bulletin and pulpit announcements for "volunteers"; rather, you will want to be sure that bellwether members of the body are personally invited and urged to come. The rest of the flock will follow their lead, in time.

You can confidently expect the ones you choose to eagerly accept the teaching provided in the workshop, for it is entirely biblical and speaks to them on a level of their deep need and desire to serve the Lord they love.

A series of sermons could serve as an introduction to the workshop. The sermons alone cannot offer opportunities for reflection, questioning, and sharing, but can lay a foundation for the workshop where these things are possible. In the appendix some available workshop materials are listed.

2. *Small group study and practice.* From the beginning of the Christian movement, there has been no better method for discipling and developing Christians than the small group. This is particularly true of special studies leading to special ministries. We can take our example from Jesus here, although small group studies reach back further than the first century. We learn from studying the New Testament that in small groups, such as with Jesus' disciples, and not in large crowds before which he preached, the foundation of the serving church was laid. In recent years there has been a renewal of small group study and ministry. There is really no substitute for it in the study of spiritual gifts. I will be saying more about this later.

3. *Spiritual gifts inventories.* This is a device, in the form of multiple-choice questions, that helps the individual scrutinize his experiences and attitudes. Such a procedure for uncovering experiences and cognitive phenomena is not without antecedent. We all know the value of testing for intellectual skills and deficiencies and we readily recognize the important application of certain types of tests to ascertain levels of academic ability, vocational interests and aptitudes, emotional health and instabilities, professional proficiency and weakness, and social behavior.

Trained as I am in the science of clinical psychology, it is easy for me to see the value of applying this methodology in the process of discovering spiritual gifts. Gifts are given for human beings to use, and the use of them involves the whole person—mental, physical, social, and spiritual. The gifts are not phenomena that manifest themselves only through some spiritual medium or supraphysical means. The religious experience that is basic to the Christian faith is not something that transcends human nature. To be sure, it is something that changes human nature (2 Cor. 5:17), but it does not ignore or bypass it. The spiritual does not stand apart from the mental and physical. We are unitary beings with various categories of thinking, willing, and feeling. The manifestation of the presence of God (Holy Spirit) in and through the life of a person is not something that is untouched by or unrelated to the emotional, social, and motivational aspects of behavior.

Since psychology studies human behavior in all of its aspects, we do well to utilize its methods of research to gain assistance in understanding Christian human behavior. One of those methods is the self-reporting inventory, a means of reporting one's history of feelings, interests, and attitudes. I look on it as a short-cut toward the discovery of powers within our potential that have before remained unknown to us, those dimensions of our personality that are vital in the influence we could exert upon others.

Another value of an inventory is to reduce the number of possible gifts we might have to a manageable few so that we can begin to experiment and ultimately discover our gift(s). In our study of the subject so far we have uncovered some twenty-seven gifts. To the person who is just being introduced to the subject and the possibilities, this can be overwhelming. Where does he begin? He may wonder, *How long will it take me to experiment with that many before I find the gift God has for me?* The inventory will produce a hierarchy of scores based on experiences, feelings, and desires that can help the individual begin a meaningful experimentation. The principle is to experiment with as many as possible; the inventory assists in choosing where to begin. (The reader will find several inventories briefly described, and the address for each, in the Appendix. I recommend all of the inventories; the individual should select the one or two from the list that seem best to suit his situation.)

Once an inventory is completed, the individual will discover in which gifts he scores well, and in which ones he scores poorly. In most cases, the top scores are the significant ones. However, if he has answered some questions from the standpoint of natural talents, rather than what he understands as the Holy Spirit's motivation, he could be misled. For this reason, it is absolutely necessary to view the results of an inventory as only one experiment in the whole process. When he discovers his gift—he may "stumble" onto it— there will come the outward and visible manifestation of the inward, spiritual grace. The significance of a spiritual gift is always in its use, never in its possession.

If much has been said here about the value and use of the spiritual gifts inventory, it is because I have found it to be the turning point in many peoples' lives, giving them a place to begin. While the study of what the Bible has to say about spiritual gifts is the basic interest and foundation for further consideration, I have found that the results of an inventory ignite the individual's fervent interest in exploring the subject further. Once a person realizes the possibility of an intimate reality of the presence of the Holy Spirit in the form of a ministry gift, he wants to carry out his search to its conclusion. His level of enthusiasm reaches such a high because of the inventory that something more must be added to channel it to fruitful ends. Thus, the discovery group that follows. *I do not* recommend taking an inventory without the following activity.

4. *Spiritual gifts discovery group.* This is one of the most important and meaningful steps in discovering one's gift. It is based on a principle I have discovered to be a very large part of the essence of the Christian life: For one's salvation, a relationship to Christ is absolute, and is absolutely relational. Apart from Christ there is no wholeness, and this wholeness is lived out in relations with others. This applies to spiritual gifts in this way: The gift is given not only as a favor from God, but also as a means of discovering one's identity and function (ministry) in the body of Christ. The discovery group works in the following manner:

a) The first phase is to group together by gift all those who scored highest for the particular gift—serving, mercy, administration, hospitality, and so on. This group should be no larger than twelve and no smaller than four. A contract is made among them to meet weekly for only an hour at a time. At the meetings each shares with the group his reasons for answering the questions as he did. It is very important that this sharing run its course and that all members are satisfied with the hierarchy of the gift's score. In the process of a deep and intimate sharing, some persons may discover that they misread or misinterpreted the questions and that, after all, this isn't their gift. Likewise, it is to be expected that some will be confirmed in their search and gain assurance that one in particular is their gift. This phase could take as many as four to eight weeks and should not be hurried.

b) Next, those who are reasonably confident of a certain gift should continue to meet together and study the passages of Scripture related to the particular gift. A suggested method of study here is simply to take turns at reading aloud the passages and pause for reflection and prayer. I suggest that only the Bible be used at first, until all biblical references (found in the chapters on behavioral characteristics) are read and reflected upon. Then, of course, it would be helpful to acquire a good book that examines the same biblical passages. I suggest that only the gift that brought the group together be studied during this phase.

c) The third phase is to study together the behavioral characteristics and determine whether or not they fit or match the experiences of those in the group. It would be helpful here to share other behavioral characteristics which I have not listed. It is my contention that universal characteristics can be identified with certain gifts. An example of this is the way each member of a person's physical body characteristically behaves. Eyes do not behave as ears, nor do ears as eyes. Feet do not act as hands, and hands do not behave as feet. As each member of the human body has its own unique behavioral characteristics, each gift God has given for ministering has its unique behavior. From one person to the next—each having the same gift—there should be some common characteristics, if not in quantity or intensity, in quality and results.

d) If the members of the group have agreed by this time that they have possibly discovered their gift, it shouldn't be too difficult for them to recognize the same in others outside their study group. In this phase, they deliberately look for "their" gift in other members of the church.

I suggest they begin by looking at members whom they know personally, and see if they recognize in them the characteristics of the gift. When they do recognize such, let them approach the person and invite him or her to a session.

In the meeting, the one who extended the invitation would reveal to the person what the group has discovered about the presence of a spiritual gift, and that they all had agreed, according to their observations, that this gift may also reside in the visitor's life. An interesting and profitable discussion should ensue.

Such a meeting could serve as an introduction for the person to attend a future workshop. It will certainly set that person to thinking of what he or she had not been aware of previously.

e) This done, the individuals should leave this group and join with others to consider the next gift in numerical rank on their spiritual gifts inventory. It is highly unlikely that the same persons will be together. In the new group, they go through steps a) through d) again. I do not advise that a person be in more than one group at one time, due to the difficulty in sorting out feelings and practice.

In conclusion, if study groups cannot be quickly scheduled, it is important that immediate opportunities be offered by the pastor and other church leaders for these people to begin testing their prospective gifts in actual ministry situations. This would speed up the ultimate discovery and confirmation.

It is very important that these opportunities be fully explained to all involved. For example, if a person whose gift may be teaching is assigned to teach as a way of experimenting with the gift, class members (in an adult situation) should be made aware of what is going on and told how they can be of help. The principle is that the confirmation of the gift by the body is a must. The gift is for the benefit of the body.

Conducting a workshop or seminar on spiritual gifts can take various forms. But whatever the form, it is important to consider the level of sophistication of the participants and the stream of tradition with which they identify. Time must be allowed for adequately introducing the idea and obtaining needed materials; and don't forget follow-up. Allow for further study and experimentation for the participants.

An ample supply of materials is available: books, film-strips, 16 mm. films, and audio- and video-tapes for the pastor who wishes to conduct his own study. Many individuals have acquired expertise in the subject of gifts, but they are not as easily available as the materials. Because of this, I offer the following format for the pastor who wishes to conduct his own program of study and discovery.

1. *Get the approval of the governing body of the church.* Take the matter to the appropriate committee in the church and explain the concept that each person has a gift for ministry to be discovered. Seek their approval and support for a more formal presentation to the church governing body. Let one or more members of the initial committee share the presentation with the pastor before the governing body. During this presentation, consider showing the movie "Discover Your Gifts" (described in the Appendix). Gain the approval of this body and a commitment from the members to attend the upcoming workshop.

2. *Set the date.* Well in advance, plan for a date in the church calendar. Allow time for a series of announcements and sermons related to the subject of gifts. These sermons may be on various aspects of the Holy Spirit. They would

be especially helpful if they could emphasize Paul's witness and teachings, since the study done in the seminar will lean heavily on his letters. The bibliography at the end of this book can be helpful here. Among those listed, I would particularly point out Kenneth Kinghorn's *Gifts of the Spirit,* C. Peter Wagner's *Your Spiritual Gifts Can Help Your Church Grow,* and *Unwrapping Your Spiritual Gifts,* by David Hubbard.

3. *Begin recruiting participants.* Pulpit and newsletter announcements are essential, but personal recruiting is a must. If you are a pastor, you know who really wants to give his best to God and the church. You know how people struggle to find the right place of service. It may be that you are struggling over how to guide them. Simply tell them that God has a way of breaking through to individuals when they are in a relational effort to discover his will. This study may be the very means for their discovering God's explicit plan for their ministries.

4. *Choose the kind of workshop you want.* After you have studied the subject in general and the gifts in particular, you may decide to lean heavily on the seminar approach, which is characterized by lessons or lectures that you will present, with a minimum amount of actual work for the participants. On the other hand, you may be attracted to the pure workshop type that requires a lot from the participants. This style is best illustrated by the Christian Reformed Church manual. Or you may be attracted to the video-tapes study. Still another method is to pick an appropriate book as the text and distribute copies in advance. With this method you simply review each chapter and the insights you and the participants gain. The last option I suggest is listening to cassette tapes. There are many series of these. The simple method is listening and discussing. Once you have chosen the style that suits you, order the materials.

How To Conduct a Spiritual Gifts Workshop

The time has arrived. You have chosen the method you want to follow, and the participants have arrived. I am going to assume that you have chosen a mix between the seminar and workshop types. This is my favorite method, and it easily utilizes the chapters of this book. The following is a suggested outline.

MODULE ONE: WHY STUDY SPIRITUAL GIFTS?

1. First hour:
   a) (5 min.) Convene for devotions.
   b) (10 min.) Break up into small groups and assign each person to share why he or she is involved and give at least one expectation.
   c) (10 min.) With all together again, the leader will ask for brief reports from the small groups.
   d) (10 min.) Pass out sheets of blank paper and ask each person to write down as many of the spiritual gifts he or she can name. Take these up.
   e) (10 min.) Leader write (or call out for someone else to write on board or on flipchart) all the gifts reported on the papers.
   f) (15 min.) Leader will describe conditions that prevail in the church, community, and world that cry out for empowered Christians, and say how the gifts contribute to the empowerment. (See the Introduction of this book.)

2. Second hour:
   a) (15 min.) Introduce basic biblical passages: Romans 12:6–9; 1 Corinthians 12:8–10, 28; Ephesians 4:11; 1 Peter 4:11. As these are read aloud, have someone put a check mark next to gifts listed on the board or flipchart.
   b) (15 min.) Introduce the principles related to spiritual gifts (chapter 1).

c) (25 min.) Show the movie, "Discover Your Gifts." This will dramatize the whys, hows, and whats in process toward discovery of gifts.

(Make your workshop fit your own style. The above can be altered. Some may want to eliminate the "icebreaker" element in 1.b to give more time to point 1.f, which may require more.)

MODULE TWO: WHAT ARE THE SPIRITUAL GIFTS?
1. First hour:
a) (20 min.) The Source of Spiritual Gifts. (See chapter 2; see also *The Holy Spirit in the Life of the Church*, edited by Paul D. Opsahl, especially chapter 3, by William G. Rusch.
b) (20 min.) What the Gifts Are Not. (See chapter 3 of this book.) It is very important to make a distinction between a spiritual gift and a talent, acquired natural ability, developed skill, interest, role, or office.
c) (20 min.) What the Gifts Are. (See chapter 4 of this book.)
2. Second hour:
a) (10 min.) Taking a look at the "Varieties of Gifts, Services, and Results." (See chapter 5.)
b) (20 min.) Pass out sheet, "What We Have Learned So Far." Allow ten minutes for filling out and ten minutes for checking the answers. This should be designed by the leader based on how much he expects the participants to have been exposed to by this time. A model for this is in the *Discover Your Gifts* notebook, a description of which is in the Appendix.
c) (20 min.) Some illustrative results of using gifts. C. Peter Wagner's book *Your Spiritual Gifts Can*

Help Your Church Grow (see Bibliography) is full of models and examples of churches and individuals using their gifts. It is essential that some good illustrations be offered.

d) (10 min.) Instructions for filling out the inventory. Whichever inventory you choose, you will want to explain how to take it and score it before the next session. Make sure the group understands that this is designed to examine closely their "body life" history—how they have related to the church in attitude and action. If there is no history, the participant should be encouraged to fantasize, but only in relationship to the body of Christ.

MODULE THREE: DISCOVERING YOUR SPIRITUAL GIFT

1. First hour:

a) (20 min.) Discovery through OBEDIENCE (see chapter 7), nine steps toward discovering your spiritual gift(s).

b) (10 min.) Review and discussion of inventory. Be sure to review section 3, chapter 11 of this book.

c) (20 min.) Distribute sheet with blanks for information you want back from their inventory. I usually ask for name, address, and telephone number; included are six lines for listing the top six gifts according to the scoring; lines on which each is asked to list current and formerly held jobs in church. Leader sorts these by highest scores during break.

2. Second hour:

a) (20 min.) Divide into groups based on common gifts. During the break period between the first and second hour, leader sorts the lists to assist in getting persons together with common gifts. Let them discuss personal experiences that influenced them in answering the questions as they did.

b) (10 min.) Reports of interesting experiences from each group.

c) (15 min.) For the gifts that appeared most frequently in the scoring, review behavioral characteristics found in chapters 6–9.

d) (15 min.) Organize participants into small groups for continued studies based on the plan in section 4, chapter 11, "Spiritual Gifts Discovery Group." Explain the plan thoroughly.

The Workshop is only an introduction. For it to become anything more, the follow-up group study is essential.

APPENDIX

A. Workshops in Notebook Form

1. *Spiritual Gifts and Church Growth,* published and marketed by Charles E. Fuller Institute of Evangelism and Church Growth, P. O. Box 989, Pasadena, CA 91102. This notebook workshop also includes a "Mobilization Workbook" which goes beyond the discovery of gifts to the installation of persons and their gifts in places for ministry in the body of Christ. Contains a leader's guide and participant's notebook, two cassette tapes by Dr. C. Peter Wagner of Fuller Theological Seminary made "on location" while teaching; some overhead artwork for use on transparencies.

2. *Spiritual Gifts for Building the Body,* published and marketed by The Institute for American Church Growth, 150 South Los Robles, Suite #600, Pasadena, CA 91101. This is a "study integrator" which is very helpful for self- or group-study. It uses Wagner's book, *Your Spiritual Gifts Can Help Your Church Grow;* Dr. Kenneth Cain Kinghorn's book, *Gifts of the Spirit;* and *Discover Your Spiritual Gift and Use It,* by Rick Yohn, as basic texts. Accompanying cassette tapes by Charles Crow.

3. *Spiritual Gifts Workshop,* by Dr. Raymond W. Hurn, of the Church Extension Ministries, Church of the Nazarene, 6401 The Paseo, Kansas City, MO 64131. This is in notebook form, in simple format based on twenty gifts. An inventory, designed by the author, is an aid in discovering gifts. Two cassette tapes are included, one by Dr. Hurn and the other by Dr. Marris Weigelt, professor of New Testament at Nazarene Theological Seminary. The kit contains a participant's notebook and leader's guide.

4. *Discover Your Gifts* workshop notebook, published by the Christian Reformed Church, 2850 Kalamazoo Avenue, Grand Rapids, MI 49560, by far the finest document I have found on the market. Attractively printed and arranged, it contains notebook for the leader, with helpful materials in the margins, and attractive workbook for participants. Contains 36 questions most frequently asked, with answers, plus a set of transparencies and a tape of a workshop actually conducted. Includes a self-test (inventory) covering fifteen gifts and also sermon outlines which can serve as small group study and church school class lessons. Workshop is divided into six one-hour modules.

B. Inventories or Self-tests

1. *Modified Houts Questionnaire,* published and marketed by the Fuller Evangelistic Association. This was originally designed by Dr. Richard F. Houts, professor of Christian education at Ontario Bible College and later revised by C. Peter Wagner. Contains 125 statements which require one of the following descriptions as to how the statement fits experience: Much, Some, Little, or Not at All. It covers twenty-five gifts. This is my favorite inventory because it has been around a long time and has proven its worth. Institute of Evangelism and Church Growth, Box 989, Pasadena, CA 91102.

2. *The Spiritual Gifts Inventory (McMinn),* a computerized inventory designed by Gordon McMinn, Ph.D. in psychology, with the assistance of Dr. Earl Radmacher and Dr. Loren Fisher of Western Conservative Baptist Seminary. The questionnaire covers only twelve of the gifts. Its unique feature, beyond the fact that the scoring is done by computer, is that it has three sets of statements. Person tested chooses one of the three most descriptive of his experience; then, one that is least descriptive of his experience. By the time you have finished three-fourths of them, mental blisters begin to appear! There are 192 sets of state-

ments! But the SGI is worth the taking. It costs $10.00 per person (group rate of $7.50 per SGI). One should not stop with taking one of the self-tests. The Houts and McMinn questionnaires are a good combination in the quest to discover one's gifts.

3. *Gifts Analysis Questionnaire*, presented as a part of the notebook workshop by the Christian Reformed Church (see A, 4 above).
4. *Spiritual Gifts Profile*, presented as a part of the notebook workshop by the Church of the Nazarene (see A,3 above).
5. *Gifts of the Spirit Questionnaire*, by Kenneth Cain King- horn, author of the book by the same title. This can be acquired by writing Dr. Kinghorn at Asbury Theological Seminary in Wilmore, Kentucky. The book is published by Abingdon, Nashville. The questionnaire is not a part of the published book.
6. *Trenton Spiritual Gifts Analysis*, modeled after the Houts (see B, 1), includes seventeen gifts. It is designed by a Lutheran Church for other liturgical churches. Order from Charles E. Fuller Institute, P. O. Box 91990, Pasadena, CA 91109–1990.
7. *Wesley Spiritual Gifts Questionnaire*, a combination of Houts and Trenton, with five other gifts defined but not tested in the body of questions. Order from Charles E. Fuller Institute (see above for address).

C. Bookform Workshop with Questionnaire

Finding Your Spiritual Gift, by Tim Blanchard. The complete title is "A Practical Guide to Finding and Using Your Spiritual Gifts." Published by Tyndale House Publishers, Inc., Whea- ton, Illinois, this is a manual that does several things: brief biblical study of thirteen gifts, contains the McMinn inven- tory (see B,2 of Appendix), has section for others' assessment of one's characteristics related to gifts, contains brief descrip- tions of behavioral characteristics related to practicing a gift, and helps for planning a spiritual gifts seminar or workshop.

D. Video and Cassette Tapes on Spiritual Gifts
(Video Cassettes)
1. *Biblical Basis for Spiritual Gifts*, Dr. Kenneth Cain Kinghorn. Order from Video Leadership Ministries, P. O. Box 985, Starkville, MS 39759. (28 minutes)
2. *Biblical Principles for Spiritual Gifts*, (same as above).
3. *Discovering Your Spiritual Gifts*, (same as No. 1 above).

(Cassette Tapes)
1. *Spiritual Gifts*, Brown, Stephen. Key Life Tapes, Key Biscayne Presbyterian Church, 160 Harbor Drive, Key Biscayne, FL 33149. (Series of four tapes)
2. *Spiritual Gifts*, Radmacher, Earl D. Western Conservative Baptist Seminary, 5511 S.E. Hawthorne Blvd., Portland, OR 97215. (Four 90-minute cassettes with two study booklets)
3. *God's Children—Gifted for Ministry*, Stanley, Charles F. In Touch Ministries, P. O. Box 7900, Atlanta, GA 30357. This is a series of sermons by Dr. Stanley preached on television.

E. Movies (16mm.) About Spiritual Gifts
1. *Discover Your Gifts.* A challenge to Christians to discover their gifts and use them through the church. When Chuck Bradley's overworked pastor is stricken with a heart attack while jogging with Chuck, Chuck begins soliciting members for his church's class on discovering gifts for ministry. Chuck finds that he has the gift of evangelism and leads his doctor friend to Christ. This movie is very well done; $39.00 for rental. May be secured from The Institute for American Church Growth, 709 E. Colorado Boulevard, Suite 150, Pasadena, CA 91101.

BIBLIOGRAPHY

Note: Although I did not directly quote any of these authors, I must confess gratitude and deep indebtedness to them for their inspiration. After one reads scores of books on a subject and begins writing his own thoughts, it would be impossible to sort out what may or may not be original thinking. The best he can do and, perhaps, the most honest, is to give credit to all whom he has read and hope he may be able to contribute additional insight. The listing below is a selective bibliography, based mainly on mainline church authors. Good theology and reasonable applications of charismata is desperately needed in the middle or mainline churches.

Banks, Paul. *Paul's Idea of Community.* Grand Rapids: Eerdmans, 1980.

Barclay, William. *The Letters to the Corinthians.* Philadelphia: Westminster, 1975.

———. *The Letters to Galatians and Ephesians.* Philadelphia: Westminster, 1975.

———. *The Letters to the Romans.* Philadelphia: Westminster, 1976.

Bennett, Dennis and Rita. *The Holy Spirit and You.* Plainfield, N.J.: Logos, 1971.

Blanchard, Tim. *A Practical Guide to Finding and Using Your Spiritual Gifts.* Wheaton: Tyndale House, 1983.

Carter, Charles W. *The Person and Ministry of The Holy Spirit. A Wesleyan Perspective.* Grand Rapids: Baker, 1977.

Hubbard, David A. *Unwrapping Your Spiritual Gifts.* Waco: Word, 1985.

Kelsey, Morgan. *Tongue Speaking: The History and Meaning of the Charismatic Experience.* New York: Crossroad, 1981.

Kinghorn, Kenneth Cain. *Gifts of the Spirit.* Nashville: Abingdon, 1976.

Kirkpatrick, Dow, ed. *The Holy Spirit.* Nashville: Tidings, 1974.

Koenig, John. *Charismata: God's Gifts for God's People.* Philadelphia: Westminster, 1978.

Kuhn, Barbara. *The Whole Lay Ministry Catalog.* New York: Seabury, 1979.

Küng, Hans. *The Church.* New York: Doubleday, 1976.

Laurentin, Rene. *Catholic Pentecostalism.* Garden City: Doubleday, 1977.

MacGorman, J. W. *The Gifts of the Spirit.* Nashville: Broadman, 1980.

Minear, Paul S. *Images of the Church in the New Testament.* Philadelphia: Westminster, 1970.

Moltmann, Jurgen. *The Church in the Power of the Spirit.* New York: Harper and Row, 1977.

O'Connor, Elizabeth. *Eighth Day of Creation—Discovering Your Gifts and Using Them.* Waco: Word, 1984.

Ogilvie, Lloyd J. *You've Got Charisma.* Nashville: Abingdon, 1983.

Opsahl, Paul D., ed. *The Holy Spirit in the Life of the Church, from Biblical Times to the Present.* Minneapolis: Augsburg, 1978.

Schramm, Mary R. *Gifts of Grace.* Minneapolis: Augsburg, 1982.

Snyder, Howard A. *The Problem of Wineskins: Church Renewal in a Technological Age.* Downers Grove: InterVarsity, 1975.

————. *The Community of the King.* Downers Grove: InterVarsity, 1977.

————. *The Radical Wesley.* Downers Grove: InterVarsity, 1980.

Stedman, Ray C. *Body Life* (rev. ed.). Glendale: Regal, 1979.

Stott, John R. W. *God's New Society: The Message of Ephesians.* Downers Grove: InterVarsity, 1980.

Strong, James. *Strong's Exhaustive Concordance of the Bible* (rev. ed.). Nashville: Abingdon, 1980.

Sweet, Leonard I. *New Life in the Spirit.* Philadelphia: Westminster, 1982.

Thayer, Joseph H. *Greek-English Lexicon of the New Testament.* Grand Rapids: Baker, 1977.

Thielicke, Helmut. *The Evangelical Faith, Vol. 3.* Grand Rapids: Eerdmans, 1982.

Tuttle, Robert G., Jr. *The Partakers.* Nashville, Abingdon: 1974.

Wagner, C. Peter. *Your Spiritual Gifts Can Help Your Church Grow.* Ventura: Regal, 1982.

Yohn, Rick. *Discover Your Spiritual Gift and Use It.* Wheaton: Tyndale, 1982.